CAMBRIDGE ASSIGNMENTS IN MUSIC

History of Music

New Edition

ROY BENNETT

CAMBRIDGE
UNIVERSITY PRESS

Contents

What is 'style' in music?

In writing a piece of music, a composer is combining together several important musical elements — what we might describe as the basic 'ingredients' of music. These include:

melody · harmony · rhythm · timbre · form · texture

We use the word **style** to describe the characteristic manner in which composers – of different times and of various countries – combine and present these basic ingredients in their music. As we shall find, composers of each period in the history of music make use of most, if not all, of these ingredients (though early Medieval music makes no use of harmony; and in some 20th-century compositions there may be no melody to speak of).

It is in fact the special way in which these musical ingredients are treated, balanced and combined which brings to any composition the distinctive 'flavour' or style of its particular period – and, at the same time, provides characteristic 'fingerprints' by which we may identify the musical style of individual composers.

PERIODS OF MUSICAL HISTORY

We can divide the history of music into separate periods of time, each identified by its own particular style. Of course, musical style does not change overnight. It is a gradual process, often with different styles overlapping so that a 'new' style emerges from within the 'old'. Because of this, musicians rarely agree about the choice of dates to mark the beginning and end of each period, or even which name should be used to describe its musical style. Here, however, is one way of dividing the history of western music into six main periods, with dates suggested for each one:

Medieval music	to about 1450
Renaissance music	1450 – 1600
Baroque music	1600 – 1750
Classical music	1750 – 1810
19th-century Romanticism	1810 – 1910
20th-century music	1900 onwards

Before investigating the style of each of these musical periods, let us take a closer look at the six basic ingredients of music:

MELODY

To most people, **melody** is the most important ingredient in a piece of music. Everyone, of course, knows what a melody is – yet it is not easy to give a precise definition of this very familiar musical word. One dictionary of music suggests: 'a series of notes of different pitch, organised and given shape to make musical sense to the listener'. But reaction to melody is a very personal matter. What may make 'musical sense' to one listener may prove unacceptable to another; and what one person considers to be an interesting, even beautiful, melody may leave someone else quite unmoved.

HARMONY

Harmony is heard when two or more notes of different pitch are sounded at the same time, producing a chord. Chords are of two kinds: concords, in which the notes agree with each other; and discords, in which (to a greater or lesser extent) the notes 'disagree', and so build up tension. We use the word 'harmony' in two ways: to refer to the choice of notes which make up an individual chord; or, in a broader sense, to describe the overall flow or progression of chords throughout a composition.

RHYTHM

The word **rhythm** is used to describe the ways in which a composer groups together musical sounds, mainly with regard to duration (the lengths of different sounds in relation to each other) and stress or accent. Going along in the background (either heard, or merely felt) there will be a regular beat – the steady 'pulse' or 'heart-beat' of the music, against which the ear measures rhythm.

TIMBRE

Each instrument has its own special sound quality, or 'tone-colour'. The characteristic sound of a trumpet, for instance, makes it possible for us to recognise it immediately – to tell the difference between a trumpet and, say, a violin. We call this special sound quality the **timbre** of an instrument. A composer may blend timbres together – for instance, the instruments of the string section of the orchestra, or instruments with rich, dark tone-colours such as cor anglais, cellos and bassoons; or he may choose to contrast the timbres of certain instruments so that the sounds stand out sharply one from another – for example, the bright penetrating sounds of piccolo, high clarinet, muted trumpet and xylophone, perhaps against a more sombre background of low brass and strings.

FORM

We use the word **form** to describe the basic plan or design which a composer may use to shape and build up a piece of music. There are many kinds of musical forms and designs – composers using different methods at different periods in the history of music.

TEXTURE

Some pieces of music present a rather dense sound: rich, and smoothly flowing. Other pieces may have a thinner, sparser sound, sometimes producing an effect which is jagged or spiky. To describe this aspect of music we use the word **texture**, likening the way the sounds are woven together in a musical composition to the way in which threads are woven in a piece of fabric. There are three basic ways in which a composer may weave the 'fabric' of his music:

- **monophonic** texture: a single melodic line entirely without supporting harmonies of any kind;
- **polyphonic** texture: two or more melodic lines weaving along at the same time (this is also sometimes described as **contrapuntal** texture);
- **homophonic** texture: a single melody heard against a (usually) chordal accompaniment with basically the same rhythm moving in all the parts at the same time.

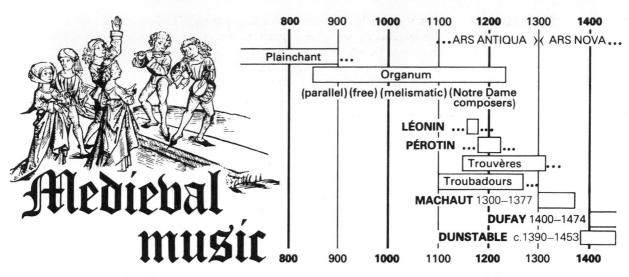

Medieval music

PLAINSONG

The earliest music we know, both sacred and secular ('non-sacred'), consists of a single melodic line – the kind of texture we call monophonic. Early church music, known as plainsong or plainchant, was sung without accompaniment. These flowing melodies, usually lying within the range of one octave, move smoothly in steps rather than by leaps; and the rhythms are irregular, freely following the natural rhythms and stresses of the Latin words to which this music is sung. Some chants are sung antiphonally – one choir singing in alternation with another. Others are sung in response style, with one or more soloists answered by the full choir. Plainsong is still in regular use today in many churches and abbeys.

1 😐

[Solo] Be - ne - di ca - mus Do _____ mi - no.
[Choir] De _____ o gra _____ ti - as.
(Let us bless the Lord. Thanks be to God.)

Modes

Early music (in fact, music up to the 17th century) used a special system of scales called **modes**. You can play a mode on the piano by starting on a white note, say D, and going upwards step by step – but keeping to white notes only. If you try this, beginning on other notes, you will find that no two modes have the same arrangement of tones and semitones. The mode in which a melody is written can be identified by its **final** – the note on which it begins and ends; and by the **range** of the melody – the lowest note to the highest.

Each medieval mode existed in two forms: an 'authentic' form (for example, D to D – Dorian mode) and a 'plagal' form – the same mode with the same final, but with a range lying a fourth lower. In this case, the mode added 'hypo' to the beginning of its name (for example, range A to A but with final note D – Hypodorian mode):

Dorian mode (authentic)	Phrygian	Lydian	Mixolydian	Aeolian	Ionian
(final)					

Hypodorian mode (plagal)

Assignment 1

Listen to *Benedicamus Domino* (the music for this is on page 5).

1   What is the range of this chant (lowest note to highest)?
2   Which note is the *final*?
3   In which mode is this melody?
4   Between which notes do semitones occur in this mode?

PARALLEL ORGANUM

The earliest music in polyphonic texture (that is, with two or more melodic lines weaving together) dates from the 9th century. At that time, composers began a long series of experiments whose aim was to embellish or elaborate some plainchants by adding one or more extra voice-lines. Music in this style is called **organum**. In the earliest kind, called 'parallel organum', the organal voice (the added part) merely duplicates the principal voice (which sings the original plainchant) at an interval of either a fourth or a fifth below:

1 🎧

[principal voice]
[organal voice]

Sit glo-ri-a Do-mi-ni, in sae-cu-la lae-ta-bi-tur Do-mi-nus in o-pe-ri-bus su-is.
(May the glory of the Lord endure for ever: the Lord shall rejoice in his works.)

This bare, rather stark sound was often made richer by duplicating one or both of these voice-lines at the octave.

FREE ORGANUM

During the next two centuries, composers took gradual steps to free the organal voice from this rigid copying of the principal voice. By the 11th century, besides parallel motion, the organal voice also used contrary motion (rising as the principal voice fell, and vice versa), oblique motion (keeping the same note as the principal voice moved) and similar motion (taking the same direction but not keeping exactly the same distance apart). In this 'free organum', the organal voice is now above the principal voice. It is still added mainly in note-against-note style – but notice that in this piece there are three occasions when the organal voice-part has two notes to sing above a single note in the principal voice-part:

1 🎧

[organal voice]
[principal voice]

1 Re-gi re-gum glo - ri-o-so 3 As-sis-tunt in pa-la-ti-o   5 Be-ne-di-ca-mus Do - mi - no
2 Pe-trus et Pau-lus   se-du-lo 4 Su-per-ni re-gis ju-bi-lo
(By the glorious King of kings Peter and Paul stand faithfully in His palace.
With praise to the highest King let us bless the Lord.)

MELISMATIC ORGANUM

Early in the 12th century, this steady note-against-note style was abandoned altogether. Instead, the principal voice drew out the notes of the chant in long values. The principal voice now became known as the **tenor** (from Latin, *tenere*, to hold). Above these long-held tenor notes, a higher voice moved freely in smoothly flowing notes of shorter value. A melodious flourish of notes sung to a single syllable is called a **melisma** – so this type of organum is known as 'melismatic organum'. The tenor of this next piece is taken from the chant *Benedicamus Domino* (printed on page 5):

1

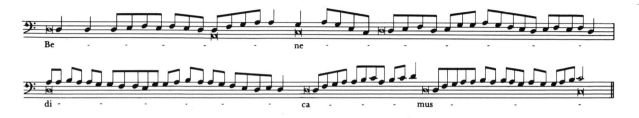

Be - - - - - ne - - - - - - - - - - - - -

di - - - - - ca - - mus - - - -

Assignment 2

A Listen again to the free organum: *Regi regum* (page 6).
 1 Which intervals (distances between the voices) are most common?
 2 Find places in this organum where the voices move in
  (a) parallel motion   (c) oblique motion
  (b) contrary motion   (d) similar motion
B In which kind of organum described so far does the organal voice move most freely against the principal voice?

ORGANUM AT NOTRE DAME

Later in the 12th century, Paris became a very important centre of musical activity when the construction of Notre Dame Cathedral was begun in 1163. Here, in the music of a group of composers called the 'Notre Dame School', the writing of organa (the plural of the word organum) reached its most elaborate and impressive stage. Only two of these composers are known to us by name: Léonin, who was the first choir-master of the cathedral; and his successor, Pérotin, who worked there from about 1180 to around 1225.

The cathedral of Notre Dame, Paris. Construction was begun in 1163, and the cathedral was consecrated in 1182.

Léonin

Léonin composed many organa based on chants belonging to important festivals of the church year, such as Christmas or Easter. Here is how a typical organum in his style would be composed:

Choosing a suitable chant – for example *Benedicamus Domino* – the composer would take that part of the chant which had only one or two notes to each syllable (Be-ne-di-ca-mus) as his *tenor*, spinning out the notes into extremely long values – so long, in fact, that it is likely that Notre Dame tenors were helped, or even replaced, by instruments such as organ or bells. Above this, the composer would write a solo (now called *duplum*, 'second part') in quicker notes, as earlier composers had done in melismatic organum – but with one important difference. In Notre Dame organa, the upper parts are **measured** (arranged in precise units of musical time) with the voices weaving dance-like phrases based on rhythm-patterns, all in triple time, which were in fact borrowed from poetry.

DISCANT STYLE AND THE CLAUSULA

When, however, the composer came to a segment of the original chant which offered a melisma ('Do.... mi-no') he would set the tenor moving in rhythm also, using up notes in this segment of the chant at a faster rate. This style of writing was known as **discant**, and the section of an organum where it occurred was called a **clausula**. Here, the tenor-notes would usually be arranged according to a short rhythmic pattern, repeated over and over throughout the clausula.

Only the solo portions of the original chant were set in polyphony for solo voices. Any portions of the chant originally sung by the choir would be performed as before – unmeasured, and in unison.

1 ⬚

Organum duplum (two-voice organum): *Benedicamus Domino* *(in the style of Léonin)*

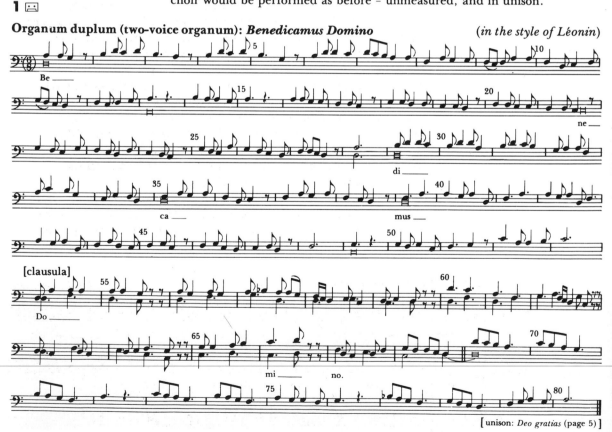

[unison: *Deo gratias* (page 5)]

8

Assignment 3
Although the phrases in the upper part of this organum duplum (or two-voice organum) vary in length, notice how the composer organises them to give shape to the line by using certain musical 'devices':
(a)   by repeating the same rhythmic pattern (bars 2-3 and 4-5)
(b)   by repeating the same snatch of melody (bars 39-40 and 41-42)
(c)   by using **sequence** – a snatch of melody immediately repeated, but at a slightly higher or lower pitch (bars 16-17, 18-19 and 20-21)
As you listen to this organum, make a note of places where you hear other examples of each of these musical devices.

Pérotin
Pérotin, who succeeded Léonin as choir-master at Notre Dame, revised many of the earlier organa, making additions and alterations to bring them more up-to-date in style. To an organum duplum he might add a third part (**triplum**) and even a fourth (**quadruplum**). He also composed many clausulae – some to be substituted for those already found in earlier organa, some to be performed as separate pieces.

Assignment 4
Listen to a record of an organum by Pérotin. Notice how the voices now weave a more intricate texture, and how the piece is structured in vast arches of sound. This is fitting music for the impressive surroundings in which it was originally intended to be sung!

MOTETS
In the 13th century, the upper parts of many clausulae were provided with independent words. The duplum now became known as the 'motetus' (from the French, *mots*, meaning 'words') and so began a very popular type of piece called the **motet**. Many motets were for performance outside church, and so were provided with secular words. Above a clausula, perhaps from a two-voice organum, a third part (**triplum**) might be added in quicker notes. This would have quite independent words – sometimes even in another language. Strangely, the triplum was required to fit musically with either the tenor (now played, rather than sung), or the duplum – but not necessarily both. This resulted at times in some crunching discords! Building up a piece like this in successive layers, sometimes each layer by a different composer, is very typical of Medieval music.

Here is the opening of a 13th-century motet, based on the clausula of the two-voice organum printed opposite. Words of a sad love-poem have been added to the duplum. Then a new triplum added with words
1 🔲 of a more cheerful love-poem. Both poems are in French.

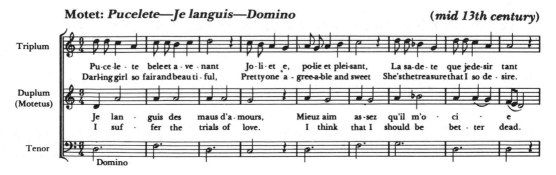

Motet: *Pucelete—Je languis—Domino*   (*mid 13th century*)

Triplum

Pu-ce-le - te beleet a - ve - nant   Jo-li-et e, po-lie et plei-sant,   La sa-de-te que jede-sir tant
Dar-ling girl so fair and beau ti - ful,   Pretty one a - gree-a-ble and sweet   She's the treasure that I so de - sire.

Duplum (Motetus)

Je lan - guis des maus d'a-mours,   Mieuz aim as-sez qu'il m'o - ci - e
I suf - fer the trials of love.   I think that I should be bet - ter dead.

Tenor

Domino

9

Conductus

Another kind of piece which became popular with Notre Dame composers was the **conductus.** This was a processional piece, sung to accompany the priest – to 'conduct' him – in his movements about the church. In writing a conductus, instead of borrowing a tenor-part from plainchant, the composer freely invented his own. Above this tenor he added one, two, or even three, further voice-parts, mainly in note-against-note style. Unlike the motet, a conductus used exactly the same text in all the voice-parts. An interesting musical device used by composers, particularly in a conductus, was **voice-exchange.** Scraps of tune, or even whole phrases, are exchanged between the voice-parts. For example, while one voice is singing **A B**, another voice, at the same time, is singing **B A**.

Voice-exchange

voice 1:	phrase **A**	phrase **B**
voice 2:	phrase **B**	phrase **A**

1 🖭

Like the motet, the conductus moved outside the church to become a secular piece. Listen to *Veris ad imperia* – a joyful three-voice conductus in praise of Spring, involving voice-exchange.

Assignment 5

Listen again to the motet *Pucelete – Je languis – Domino*, followed by the conductus *Veris ad imperia*. Afterwards, give three ways in which the motet is different in style from the conductus.

MEDIEVAL SONGS AND DANCES

1 🖭

Most Medieval songs and dances are monophonic (single-line texture). During the 12th and 13th centuries a great many songs were composed by the **troubadours**, the aristocratic poet-musicians of southern France, and the **trouvères**, their counterparts in the north. Both these words are connected with the modern French word *trouver*, which means 'to find' – and so troubadours and trouvères were 'finders', or inventors, of poems and melodies.

These melodies are written down in a way which gives a clear idea of pitch, but not of actual note-values. We must guess these from the natural rhythms of the words. No indication is given of instruments which may have joined in, but it is unlikely that these songs were performed without accompaniment. There may also have been an instrumental introduction, and interludes played between verses.

Listen to some troubadour and trouvère songs. For example, the song by the troubadour Raimbault de Vacqueiras called *Kalenda Maya*, which can be sung in a vigorous dance-rhythm: 'The first of May, but neither leaf nor flower nor birdsong can give me pleasure till I receive a message from my love . . .'

And the trouvère song, *C'est la fin*, in which the anonymous poet-musician is in sadder mood: 'This is the end. No matter what may be said, I shall love . . .'

2 🖭

The most popular kinds of Medieval dance were the **estampie** (possibly a 'stamping dance') and the **saltarello** (a 'jumping dance'). They are built up in sections, each one repeated – the first time ending 'ouvert' (open), the second time 'clos' (closed). A dance might be played entirely by one or two instruments; or by a larger group, with one or two soloists beginning each section, then the rest all joining in. Here is a 13th-century French court dance called a 'ductia', which is a rather short kind of estampie:

A *Danse Royale* (13th century)

B

C

MEDIEVAL INSTRUMENTS

Instruments which may have joined in these songs and dances include:

Pipe and tabor   a pipe and a two-headed drum, played by one person

Shawm   double-reed instrument, ancestor of the oboe; powerful tone

Cornett   of ivory or wood bound with leather; it had a trumpet-like mouthpiece, but finger-holes like a recorder

Organ   besides the church organ there was also the portative organ, small, with few notes, and able to be carried as it was played

Chime bells   graded in size and pitch; struck with metal hammers

Citole   its four brass strings were plucked

Harp   smaller than the modern harp and with far fewer strings

Fiddle or vielle   slightly larger than the modern viola; a flatter bridge allowed more than one string to be played at once

Rebec   pear-shaped bowed instrument with usually three strings

Hurdy-gurdy   the strings, 'stopped' by sliders pressed down by the fingers, were vibrated by a rotating wheel turned by a handle

Psaltery   the strings were plucked with quills, one in each hand

Also: recorders of various sizes; the soft-voiced Medieval flute; the long, straight Medieval trumpet; lute; bagpipes; and percussion instruments such as cymbals, triangle, and various kinds of drum.

medieval lute

pipe and tabor

cornett

fiddle

citole

rebec

psaltery

hurdy-gurdy

shawm

Assignment 6   Listen to records of other Medieval songs and dances, identifying the sounds of as many instruments which take part as you can.

ARS NOVA
(THE NEW ART)

At three points in the history of music, occurring roughly 300 years apart, we find sudden important changes taking place in musical style. It is interesting to notice that on each of these occasions the music was described in some way as 'new'. (c = *circa* meaning 'about')

  c1300 – **Ars Nova** (The New Art)
  c1600 – **Le Nuove Musiche** (The New Music)
  c1900 – **The New Music**

When the name **Ars Nova** was given to music composed at the beginning of the 14th century in France and Italy, musicians then began to refer to the style of the previous century as **Ars Antiqua** (Old Art).

Ars Nova style is rather more polished and expressive. Rhythms are more flexible, more adventurous; and the counterpoint (or polyphony) weaves more freely. But although the harmony is generally fuller, phrases still tend to begin and end with rather bare-sounding chords consisting of fifths, fourths and octaves.

Guillaume de Machaut
(c1300–c1377)

The greatest Ars Nova musician was the French composer, Guillaume de Machaut, who wrote a great many motets and chansons (or songs). Many of his pieces are based on borrowed plainchants, but some are freely composed, so that the music is entirely of the composer's own invention. His largest and most important composition, the *Messe de Notre Dame* (Mass of Our Lady), is in a mixture of these two styles. Machaut is the earliest composer we know to have made a complete polyphonic setting of the Mass – a type of composition which soon became of great importance, and remained so for several centuries. A Mass has five main sections: Kyrie, Gloria, Credo, Sanctus, and Agnus Dei. Here is Machaut's setting of the final part of the Sanctus – the Benedictus:

2 ▱

12

Isorhythm

This is how Machaut builds up the music of his Benedictus. First he chooses a plainchant for his tenor. This becomes a **cantus firmus** - a 'fixed song', or foundation tune, upon which he builds his music. (An earlier composer writing organum would have called this the 'principal voice'.) To this cantus firmus, Machaut applies a quite lengthy rhythmic pattern which is repeated over and over throughout the piece - rather as Notre Dame composers had treated tenor-notes in a clausula. This technique came to be known as **isorhythm** ('equal rhythm'), and each statement of the rhythmic pattern was called a **talea.** (Four taleas make up this Benedictus.) The other voice-parts are then woven above and below this tenor cantus firmus.

Hocket

Another favourite medieval technique clearly heard in this music is that known as **hocket** (a word which really means 'hiccup'!). The melody is broken up into very short phrases, even separate notes, with rests between. Hocket is usually shared between two voices or instruments, so that a lively, syncopated dialogue results.

Assignment 7

A   In what ways, do you think, is this *Benedictus* by Machaut at all similar to an organum by an Ars Antiqua composer?

B   In which bars of the music, printed opposite, is hocket used?

John Dunstable (died 1453)

In the first half of the 15th century, continental composers such as Guillaume Dufay of Burgundy admired, and even copied, the style of composers from England - John Dunstable in particular. Here is the beginning of one of Dunstable's motets, *How fair thou art*. Melody, harmony and rhythm all flow smoothly to give a rich, sonorous texture. The voice-parts, in note-against-note style, are carefully blended - any discords are planned, rather than allowed to occur by chance.

Fauxbourdon style

Particularly English is the use of **fauxbourdon** style - chains of 'six-three' chords, consisting of intervals of thirds and sixths. Thirds are noticeable, too, as melodic steps in the highest voice, often tracing notes of underlying chords. This music looks forward to the smoother, more blended texture of Renaissance style.

Dunstable's motet is not based on a tenor borrowed from plainsong, but is freely composed. The words are from the Song of Solomon in the Bible.

The main characteristics of Medieval music

1 Use of modes.
2 Monophonic textures: plainsong – free-flowing unaccompanied melody; secular songs and brightly rhythmic dances.
3 Polyphonic textures: organum – elaboration of existing plainchants; motets – composed by adding successive layers of melody and words one above another, sometimes clashing to form strong discords.
4 Many compositions based on a cantus firmus borrowed from plainsong; but some pieces freely composed (for example, conductus).
5 Ars Antiqua rhythms based on regular patterns borrowed from poetry; but Ars Nova rhythms more flexible and adventurous.
6 A tendency to contrast sounds, rather than blend them together.
7 The distinctive timbres (tone-qualities) of Medieval instruments.
8 Harmonic intervals most frequently heard: unison, 4th, 5th, octave; but 3rds and 6ths more noticeable later in the Medieval period.

Assignments

8 Listen to one of Machaut's chansons such as *Douce Dame Jolie*, or *Foys Porter*. Note down the main musical differences you hear between this piece and the Benedictus from his *Messe de Notre Dame*.

9 Listen to a piece by the blind Italian Ars Nova composer, Francesco Landini – for example, his *Ecco la Primavera*.
   (a) Which instruments are used to accompany the voices?
   (b) Is the texture of this music monophonic or polyphonic?
   (c) Which musical ingredients (described on pages 3 and 4) come through most vividly in this piece?

10 Write a brief description of each of the following:
   troubadours; *estampie*; contrary motion; *cantus firmus*; motet.

11 Arrange these Medieval composers in the order in which they were born:
   Dunstable; Pérotin; Léonin; Machaut.

12 A Describe the difference between monophonic and polyphonic textures.
   B From the Medieval pieces you have listened to, give examples of each of these two kinds of musical texture.

13 Make a list of the Medieval instruments you have heard, then write a short description of each one.

14 To sample some of the style and flavour of Medieval music at first hand, try a group performance of a piece such as the *Danse Royale* on page 11. Use whatever instruments you have available whose sounds are similar to any of the Medieval instruments mentioned on the same page.

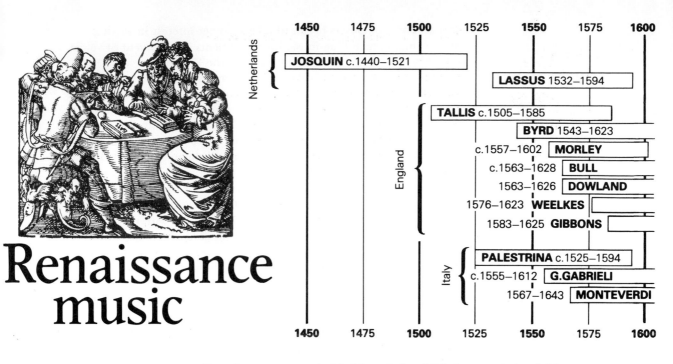

Renaissance music

Timeline 1450–1600

Netherlands
- JOSQUIN c.1440–1521
- LASSUS 1532–1594

England
- TALLIS c.1505–1585
- BYRD 1543–1623
- c.1557–1602 MORLEY
- c.1563–1628 BULL
- 1563–1626 DOWLAND
- 1576–1623 WEELKES
- 1583–1625 GIBBONS

Italy
- PALESTRINA c.1525–1594
- c.1555–1612 G.GABRIELI
- 1567–1643 MONTEVERDI

Renaissance means 'rebirth', and the chief characteristic of this period in the history of western Europe was a sharpening of interest in learning and culture, centring in particular on many of the ideas expressed by the ancient Greeks and Romans. It was also an age of exploration and discovery – the time when Columbus and other famous explorers were making their great voyages of discovery, and great advances were being made in science and astronomy.

Man explored, too, the mysteries of the human spirit and emotions, developing a keener awareness both of himself and of the world about him. Instead of accepting facts at face value, he observed and questioned – and began to reason things out for himself.

All these factors had great impact upon painters and architects, writers and composers; and, of course, upon the works they created.

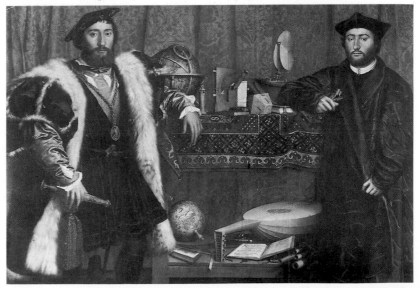

*'The Ambassadors' (1533)
by Hans Holbein
the Younger.*

Renaissance composers began to take a keener interest in writing secular music, including music for instruments independent of voices. Even so, the greatest musical treasures of the Renaissance were

CHURCH MUSIC

composed for the church. The style of Renaissance church music is described as 'choral polyphony' – contrapuntal music for one or more choirs, with several singers to each voice-part. Much of this music was intended to be sung **a cappella** (really, 'for the chapel'; and so taken to mean choral music sung without instrumental accompaniment).

Motets and masses

The main forms of church music were still the mass and the motet. These were now written in at least four voice-parts as composers began to explore the pitch-range below the tenor by writing a part we now call 'bass', so creating a fuller, richer texture. Music was still based on modes, but these were gradually used with more freedom as composers brought in more foreign notes or 'accidentals'.

Medieval techniques such as isorhythm and hocket were forgotten, but until 1550 composers still often based masses and motets on a **cantus firmus.** Now, however, rather than taking a plainchant as his foundation tune, a composer might choose a popular song instead!

One of the most noticeable differences between Medieval and Renaissance style is that of musical texture – the way in which a composer weaves the 'fabric' of his music. Whereas a Medieval composer tended to contrast the separate strands of his music one against another, a Renaissance composer aimed to blend them together. Instead of building up the texture layer after layer, he worked gradually through the piece, attending to all voice-parts simultaneously, and weaving a continuous web of polyphony.

Imitation

The key device used by composers to weave this kind of texture is called **imitation**. One voice-part introduces a snatch of tune, then is immediately imitated, or copied, by another voice-part:

Anthem: *Heare the voyce and prayer of thy servaunts*   *Thomas Tallis*

At phrase-endings where the music might come to rest and the flow be broken, the composer will often introduce fresh imitation. While a chord is held at the end of a phrase, one of the voice-parts will set off with a new tuneful idea, soon imitated by the others. In this way, the composer overlaps the strands of his texture and creates a continuous, 'seamless', musical flow.

But although, as we listen to this music, the weaving of the polyphony is the most important aspect, the Renaissance composer was becoming increasingly aware of **harmony** – the vertical framework of chords which supports the horizontal weaving of the counterpoint. And he became especially concerned with the treatment of discords. All this led to a much wider range of musical expression.

THE NETHERLANDS AND ITALY

A rather curious fact about music in the Renaissance is that, though Italy and England were to become the most important musical centres, composers who took the lead in almost every direction all came from the Netherlands. A great many of these composers settled in other countries, particularly Italy, taking up important musical posts and strongly influencing the music of native composers.

Josquin des Prez (Netherlands; c1440–1521)

Musicians of his time described Josquin as 'The Prince of Music', admiring him for the deeply emotional quality of his music and, above all, for the way in which he brought out the special meaning of the words he set. Listen to his motet, *Absalon fili mi*, which is a rich, dark-coloured setting of David's lament upon the death of his treacherous son, Absalom (as told in the Bible):

Assignment 15
A How does Josquin bring a seamless flow to the texture of this music?
B In the second half, the words (sung twice over) mean: 'Let me live no more – but let me descend into hell, weeping'. How does Josquin bring out the special meaning of these words in his music?

Palestrina (Italy; c1525–1594)

Choral polyphony soared to a peak of beauty and expressiveness during the second half of the 16th century in the music of Palestrina (Italy), Lassus (Netherlands), Byrd (England) and Victoria (Spain).

Listen to the opening of the Agnus Dei from Palestrina's *Missa Papae Marcelli* (Mass in memory of Pope Marcellus), which is not based on a cantus firmus but is freely composed. This music has a calm, serene beauty. Palestrina writes for six voice-parts, and smoothly weaves his counterpoint into a continuous, flowing texture. These two snatches of melody are heard in imitation:

A Ag-nus De - (i)   B qui tol - lis . . .

Assignment 16
First, listen to a part of the *Messe de Notre Dame* by the Medieval composer, Machaut. Then listen again to the Agnus Dei from the *Missa Papae Marcelli* by Palestrina. Describe any differences you hear in style or texture. (For instance, think about: number of voices; use of instruments; contrast or blending; harmony; rhythm and flow; use of any special techniques or musical devices.)

GERMAN CHORALES

In 16th-century Germany, where the Protestant Church led by Martin Luther was seeking ways of bringing its people into a more direct contact with God, there grew up a tradition of writing hymns to be sung in German by the whole congregation – rather than in Latin by a trained choir. The tunes were sometimes newly composed, sometimes adapted from plainchants or even popular songs. A German hymn-tune of this kind is called a **chorale**. One of the best known, still sung today, and with both words and music probably written by Luther himself, is *A safe stronghold our God is still.*

SECULAR MUSIC FOR VOICES

Alongside these developments in Renaissance church music, there was a rich flowering of secular songs – amazingly varied in style, and expressing every kind of human mood and emotion. Some are very contrapuntal in texture, making great use of imitation, while others are mainly chordal, rippling along in joyous, clear-cut rhythms borrowed from dance-music. Included among these many kinds of song are the Italian **frottola**, the German **Lied**, the Spanish **villancico**, the French **chanson**, and the Italian **madrigal**.

Assignment 17

Listen to three or four different types of song, listed below, which were popular during the Renaissance. As you listen, note down the main features of each performance. For instance, is the music:
(a) contrapuntal with use of imitation – or mainly chordal?
(b) for one or more solo voices – or several singers per voice-part?
(c) sung unaccompanied – or with instruments joining in?

Italian frottola	Josquin des Prez: *El Grillo* (The Cricket)
2 🖭	Tromboncino: *Ostinato vo' seguire* (Steadfastly, I shall pursue)
German Lied	Isaac: *Innsbruck, ich muss dich lassen* (Innsbruck, I must leave thee)
2 🖭	Senfl: *Entlaubet ist der Walde* (The wood is stripped of its leaves)
Spanish villancico	Encina: *Oy comamos y bemamos* (Let us eat and drink today)
	Alonso: *La tricotea* – a coarse drinking-song based on nonsense verse
French chanson	Passereau: *Il est bel et bon* (He is handsome and good)
	Jannequin: *Le chant de l'alouette* (The song of the lark)
Italian madrigal	Monteverdi: *O primavera* (O Spring)
2 🖭	Gesualdo: *Mille volte il di moro* (A thousand times a day I die)

ELIZABETHAN MADRIGALS

In 1588, a collection of Italian madrigals with English words was published in England. This sparked off great enthusiasm, and soon, English composers were writing their own madrigals which were performed, usually with one singer per part, in the homes of keen music-lovers everywhere. In England, there came to be three kinds of madrigal: the **'madrigal proper'**, the **ballett**, and the **ayre**.

The madrigal proper

A madrigal of this kind was 'through-composed' – that is, with fresh music to each line of text (though there is often a good deal of repetition in the words themselves). A madrigal proper is usually very contrapuntal, with much use of imitation. This makes all the voices equally important strands in the music, weaving in and out and following their own independent rhythms so that a light, springy texture is created. Words and music are closely matched, and the composer seizes every chance to introduce 'word-painting' – vivid musical illustrations of the meaning of certain words. For example, the word 'death' will be sung to a harsh discord; while a phrase such as 'merrily chased each other' will have the voices swiftly running after each other in close imitation.

1 🖼 One of the greatest Elizabethan madrigal composers was Thomas Weelkes. Listen to his madrigal proper, *As Vesta was from Latmos Hill descending*, written for six solo voices. The most vivid examples of word-painting occur in lines four to six, which run:

> To whom Diana's darlings came running down amain,
> First two by two, then three by three together,
> Leaving their goddess all alone, hasted thither.

Listen for: 'running down amain' (the voices running lightly down); 'first two by two' (voices in pairs); 'then three by three' (voices in threes); 'together' (all voices); 'all alone' (one voice only).

This madrigal is from *The Triumphs of Oriana* – a collection of 29 madrigals by 26 Elizabethan composers. 'Oriana' was the poetic name used to describe Elizabeth I. Each madrigal in the collection ends with the same two lines of verse:

> Then sang the shepherds and nymphs of Diana:
> 'Long live fair Oriana!'

The ballett

The **ballett** (the equivalent of the Italian *balletto*) was sometimes danced as well as sung. A ballett is lighter in style than a madrigal proper. It has a clear-cut, dance-like rhythm, and the texture is mainly chordal. Whereas a madrigal proper is through-composed, a ballett is strophic – two or more verses set to the same music (as in a hymn). The most noticeable feature of a ballett is the 'fa-la-la' refrain which is heard at section endings.

1 🖼 As an example of this kind of madrigal, listen to the lively ballett, *Now is the month of maying*, by Thomas Morley.

In this 16th-century illustration, five singers are accompanied by flute, cornetts, sackbuts, viols, lute and virginals.

19

An ayre by John Dowland. The music is printed in three directions so that all performers, seated around a table, might share the same copy.

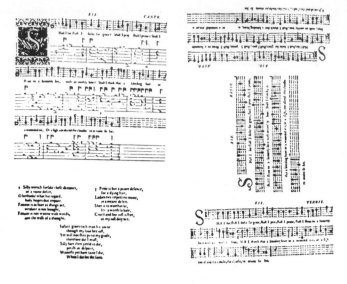

The ayre

The third kind of English madrigal was the ayre (= air, or song). Ayres were often printed on two facing pages of a book – the melody on the left, the lower parts on the right. Beneath the melody were the words and also a version of the lower parts arranged for lute.

An ayre could be performed in a variety of ways: by a solo voice with lute accompaniment; by a solo voice accompanied by other instruments such as viols; or with all the parts sung by voices, with or without instrumental accompaniment. In performance, the book was placed on a table so that singers and/or instrumentalists, seated around, were able to share the same copy.

The greatest composer of ayres was John Dowland, who was also an expert lute-player famous throughout the courts of Europe. Listen to his expressive, rather melancholy ayre, called *Flow my teares*.

1 ☐

1 ☐ **Assignment 18**

Identify the three kinds of madrigal recorded on the cassette:
1   Thomas Greaves: Come away, sweet love, and play thee
2   John Dowland: What if I never speed?
3   Thomas Vautor: Sweet Suffolk owl

As you listen to each madrigal, note down the following points:
(a)   the musicians which take part: voices unaccompanied – or with instruments joining in;
(b)   the texture: mainly chordal – or contrapuntal with imitation;
(c)   any vivid examples of 'word-painting' you are able to pick out.

CHURCH MUSIC IN ENGLAND

Besides many motets and masses composed for Catholic church services, some Elizabethan composers wrote anthems to be sung by the choir during services in Protestant churches. An anthem is the counterpart of the motet, but sung in English not Latin.

There are two kinds of anthem. **A full anthem** is sung by the choir throughout, usually unaccompanied; whereas in a **verse anthem**, verses sung by one or more soloists, accompanied by organ or viols, alternate with sections where the whole choir joins in.

Assignment 19	Listen to a full anthem, such as Thomas Tallis's *Heare the voyce and prayer of thy servaunts* (the opening is printed on page 16). Afterwards, listen to a verse anthem by Orlando Gibbons.

(a)   Which anthem is most similar in style to a motet? In what ways?

(b)   In the verse anthem by Gibbons, which type of voice sings solo? And which kinds of instrument play the accompaniment?

16TH-CENTURY VENICE

Polychoral style

At St Mark's Cathedral in Venice, there were two organ lofts and choir galleries set high up on opposite sides of the building. This gave composers the opportunity of writing for two separate choirs. Pieces in this style are described as **polychoral** – music for more than one choir. A phrase from the left is answered by the same, or perhaps a different, phrase from the right. And there are rich and splendidly powerful effects when all forces are combined.

Venetian composers were very fond of using instruments as well as voices in their church music and so would include varied groups of instruments, each group linked to its own choir. Some of the most impressive polychoral pieces are by Giovanni Gabrieli who often wrote for three, or even more, varied groups at once.

The texture of this polychoral music is a mixture of chordal style and imitative counterpoint. And there is a mixture, too, of blending and contrast – blending of sounds within the groups, but contrasts of various kinds *between* the groups. For example, in:

pitch: high-pitched sounds against sounds of lower pitch;

dynamics: *piano* (soft) against *forte* (loud);

texture: solo voices or instruments against massed groupings;

timbre: brighter timbres (or tone-colours) contrasted with darker, richer timbres.

2 ▣ **Assignment 20**

The antiphonal effects heard in polychoral music are what we might nowadays describe as 'stereophonic' — and this passing to and fro of musical ideas can be vividly captured in modern recordings.

Listen to one of Gabrieli's motets in polychoral style.

(a)   How many contrasting groups does Gabrieli use?

(b)   What are the main differences between this polychoral piece by Gabrieli and an *a cappella* composition by Palestrina?

St Mark's Cathedral, Venice, which one visitor described as 'a golden cavern encrusted with precious stones, splendidly sombre yet brilliant with all its mystery'.

MUSIC FOR INSTRUMENTS

Until the beginning of the 16th century, instruments were considered to be far less important than voices. They were used for dances, of course, and to accompany vocal music – but here they only 'doubled' (that is, played the same music as) the voices, or perhaps took over voice-parts when certain singers were unavailable. During the 16th century, however, composers took greater interest in writing music specially intended for instruments only – not only dances, but pieces purely for playing and listening.

During both the Medieval period and the Renaissance, instruments divided into two broad groups: *bas* ('low', or 'soft') instruments for music in the home; and *haut* ('high', or 'loud') instruments for music in churches, in large halls, or in the open air. A few, by the kind of sound they made, could belong to both these groups.

RENAISSANCE INSTRUMENTS

Some instruments, such as recorders, shawms and cornetts (page 11), remained popular from Medieval times. Others, like the lute, were altered and improved. And, of course, many new ones were invented.

lute the neck of the Renaissance lute was bent back; the strings were tuned in pairs, called 'courses', and the fingerboard had 'frets' (like a guitar) indicating where to press down the strings

viols had sloping shoulders and flat backs; six strings, with a fretted fingerboard; viols were held upright in front of the player rather than tucked under the chin

crumhorn a wooden cap enclosed the double reed, giving a rather soft but very reedy tone

rackett a low-pitched double-reed instrument; its great length of tube was coiled inside a cylinder which was only a foot high

sackbut a name given by the English to the early kind of trombone; the bell was less flared, giving a rounder, more mellow tone

trumpet the tube was now folded to make it more manageable; until the valve system was invented in the 19th century, the limited notes available could only be obtained by varying lip-pressure

percussion instruments included tambourine, tabor, kettle drums, side drum, triangle and cymbals

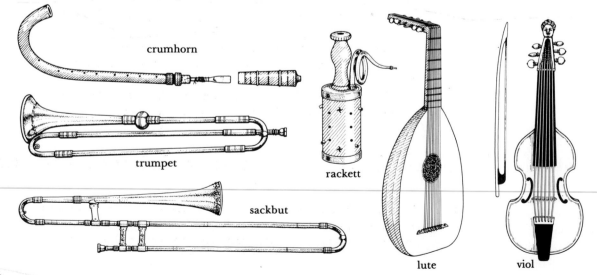

crumhorn

trumpet

rackett

sackbut

lute

viol

English Consorts

Many instruments, such as recorders, viols, shawms and crumhorns, were made in families – the same instrument in different sizes, so that there was a variety of pitch-ranges but a blending of tone within each family. In England, a family of viols or recorders was known as a 'chest', since that was how these instruments were stored when not in use. Elizabethans called a group of instruments playing together a **consort** (similar in meaning to 'concert'). Instruments from one family only – for instance, viols, or recorders – made up a **whole consort;** a **broken consort** was a mixture of instruments from different families – so that the sameness of sound was 'broken'.

Assignment 21

Listen to Elizabethan dances for broken consort, such as *Lavolto* and *La Coranto* by Thomas Morley. Which instruments make up the consort?

Dance-music was written in strong rhythms and in clear-cut phrases, often repeated, to match the various dance-steps. In other instrumental music, composers tended at first to take vocal pieces as their models, and to treat instruments rather like voices.

Canzona

Italians favoured the **canzona da sonar** (a 'song for instruments'). Many were based on actual songs, or at least written in a very similar vocal style, and built up in short, contrasted sections. Later canzonas are often for two or more contrasting groups of instruments, in the style of Venetian polychoral church music.

Ricercar

Another piece which borrowed its style from vocal music was the **ricercar.** This Italian word means 'searching out' – in this case, the possibilities of treating melodic ideas with much imitation, in similar style to a motet. More truly instrumental in style was the

Toccata

toccata for organ or harpsichord. The name comes from the Italian word 'touch', and a toccata requires some rapid finger-work.

In England, some music was considered equally suitable for singing or playing, and might be headed 'apt for voyces or vyols'. However, certain pieces were definitely intended for instruments and written to suit their special capabilities and characteristic timbres.

Variations and the ground bass

There were variations on popular tunes such as 'Greensleeves' and 'Sellenger's Round'; and variations on a **ground** – a tune repeated over and over in the bass, with changing musical material above.

Fantasia and 'In nomine'

We often find, too, the title **fantasia** – or the more Elizabethan sounding **fantasy** or **fancy**. These pieces were very contrapuntal, with a great deal of imitation between the parts. A special kind of fantasia was the **In nomine.** This was a 'cantus firmus' piece, built around the plainchant 'Gloria Tibi Trinitas' as used in the Benedictus of a mass by the composer John Taverner:

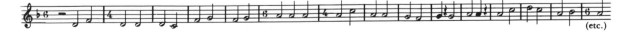

1 Listen to William Byrd's *In Nomine for Five Viols*. The cantus firmus, stretched out into long note-values, is hidden in the middle of the texture, while the other parts weave freely around it.

ELIZABETHAN KEYBOARD MUSIC

In many Elizabethan households, besides recorders, lute and viols, there would be a keyboard instrument such as the chamber organ, the clavichord (in which the strings were hit by tiny wedges of metal called 'tangents') or – most popular of all – the virginals. This was really a simple type of harpsichord with a single string to each note, the strings running parallel to the keyboard.

Most Elizabethan composers wrote pieces for virginals. They soon discovered an effective keyboard style, well suited to the instrument – spread chords and crisp decorations, swift scales and running passages. Of the many collections of pieces for the virginals, the best known are *Parthenia* – 'the first musicke that ever was printed for the Virginalls', consisting of 21 pieces by Byrd, Bull and Gibbons, and *The Fitzwilliam Virginal Book* which contains almost 300 pieces by many Elizabethan composers.

Some of these pieces are contrapuntal in style, such as fantasias. Others are arrangements of popular tunes of the day, and many are dances such as the alman and coranto. Often we find dances written in pairs, contrasted in mood and rhythm – a slow, stately pavan in two beats to a bar, followed by a spritely galliard in three beats.

1 ☺ Listen to William Byrd's pavan and galliard *The Earle of Salisbury* which was written for Elizabeth I's Secretary of State.

A favourite Elizabethan way of building up a piece was to follow each section by a decorated repeat, or variation. Giles Farnaby's *Tower Hill* is based on a popular tune which must have been cheerfully whistled by every Elizabethan errand-boy. Farnaby presents the tune in two separate sections, each followed by its own variation:

A (2 bars), **A** varied (2 bars) : **B** (4 bars), **B** varied (4 bars)

1 ☺

(etc.)

1 ☺ A composer might write a whole string of variations on a tune, gradually increasing the excitement by introducing more decorations, repeated notes, and rapid running figures passing from one hand to the other. Listen to *The King's Hunt* by John Bull, who was himself an excellent virginals player. This is **programmatic,** or descriptive, music – vividly conjuring up the sights and sounds of the hunt: jingling harnesses, galloping hooves, and hunting calls.

Assignment 22

Listen to more Elizabethan keyboard music. As you listen, identify the type of instrument used, and also the kind of piece – a dance, a set of variations, or perhaps a piece in contrapuntal style.

Virginals which may have belonged to Elizabeth I – her coat-of-arms is on the left of the keyboard. She is said to have 'plaied quite well upon the virginals – that is, for a queene...'

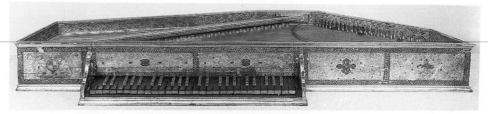

24

The main characteristics of Renaissance music

1 Music still based on modes, but these gradually treated with more freedom as more 'accidentals' creep in.

2 Richer, fuller texture, in four or more voice-parts; bass voice-part now added below tenor.

3 Blending, rather than contrasting, strands in the musical texture.

4 Harmony: a greater concern with the flow and progression of chords; a smoother treatment of discords.

5 Church music: some pieces intended for *a cappella* performance, mainly contrapuntal, with much imitation dovetailing and weaving the strands to create a continuously flowing, seamless texture; other church music accompanied by instruments – for example, polychoral pieces in antiphonal ('stereophonic') style, often involving strong musical contrasts.

6 Secular music: a rich variety of vocal pieces; dances, and also instrumental pieces – many copying vocal style but others truly suited to instruments rather than voices.

7 The characteristic timbres of Renaissance instruments – many forming families (the same instrument made in various sizes and pitches).

Assignments

23 Arrange these Medieval and Renaissance composers in the order in which they were born; then name a composition by each one:
Josquin des Prez; Gibbons; Dunstable; Palestrina; Machaut.

24 Listen to a canzona by Gabrieli for two or more contrasting groups of instruments. As you listen:
(a) identify the instruments which make up each group;
(b) note down the different kinds of musical contrast which you hear.

25 Explain each of the following:
a cappella; imitation; ayre; word-painting; *canzona*; virginals.

26 In instrumental music, particularly dances, Renaissance composers often left the actual choice of instruments to the performers themselves. Listen to dances by a Renaissance composer such as Susato, who published one collection of dances with the heading: 'pleasing and suitable for playing on all kinds of instruments'.
1 As you listen – note down the main instruments which take part.
2 Afterwards – group your instruments according to these headings: bowed strings; plucked strings; woodwind; brass; percussion.

27 Describe the difference between:
(a) a whole consort and a broken consort
(b) a cornett and a sackbut
(c) a motet and a verse anthem
(d) a madrigal proper, an ayre and a ballett

Special Assign- ment A

This assignment requires some musical detective-work! In the two boxes below you will find various kinds of music belonging to either Medieval times or the Renaissance.

Your assignment here is to listen to a varied programme made up of recordings of some of these pieces – selected from both lists, but arranged into a mixed order. As you listen, identify the style – Medieval or Renaissance – of each item, and also the kind of piece being performed.

Medieval	Renaissance
* a plainchant	* part of a mass by Palestrina
* an organum written by a Notre Dame composer	* an Elizabethan madrigal
* a troubadour song	* a polychoral motet composed for St Mark's Cathedral, Venice
* an *estampie* or *saltarello*	* a piece played by whole or broken consort
* part of Machaut's *Messe de Notre Dame*	

Before listening: Refresh your memory about the main pointers to Medieval and Renaissance style by reading the checklists on pages 14 and 25.

As you listen: Make a note of all the 'fingerprints' of style you discover in each piece – together with any other interesting details about the music.

Asking yourself the following questions will lead to the main musical 'clues' which will help you to make your identification:

(a) What kind of forces are used in the music?
Voices? Or instruments? (If so, what *kind* of instruments?)
Or perhaps a combination of both voices and instruments.
Very few performers? Or a fairly large group?

(b) What kind of piece is it? For what purpose was it composed?
Is it sacred – or secular? For worship or celebration?
Or for entertainment in homes or castles?

(c) What kind of texture does the music have?
Monophonic? Or polyphonic? Or, perhaps, mainly chordal?
Is the music built up in separate sections? Or does the texture flow continuously, perhaps closely woven with imitation?

After listening: Organise your findings by writing a brief report on each piece of music in the programme, giving:

1 The musical period – Medieval or Renaissance – during which it was composed.

2 The type of piece, with details of the forces needed to perform the music.

3 All the other 'clues' you discovered while listening to the music which helped you to make your identification.

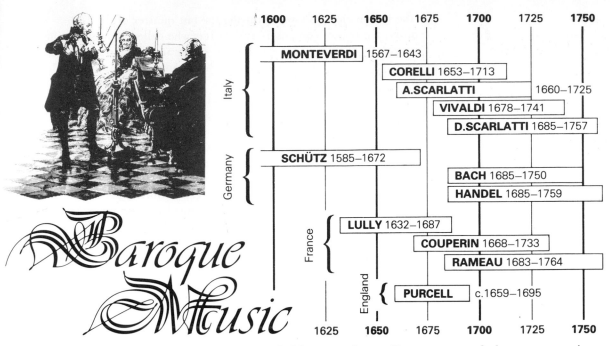

	1600	1625	1650	1675	1700	1725	1750

Italy
MONTEVERDI 1567–1643
CORELLI 1653–1713
A. SCARLATTI 1660–1725
VIVALDI 1678–1741
D. SCARLATTI 1685–1757

Germany
SCHÜTZ 1585–1672
BACH 1685–1750
HANDEL 1685–1759

France
LULLY 1632–1687
COUPERIN 1668–1733
RAMEAU 1683–1764

England
PURCELL c.1659–1695

1625	1650	1675	1700	1725	1750

'Baroque' probably comes from a Portuguese word, *barocco*, meaning an irregularly-shaped pearl or piece of jewellery. It was first used in connection with the highly ornamented style of architecture and art of the 17th century. Later on, musicians came to use the word 'Baroque' to describe the period of musical history from the birth of opera and oratorio to the death of J.S. Bach.

It was during the 17th century that the system of modes finally crumbled away. Composers had grown accustomed to sharpening a note here and flattening a note there, with the result that modes lost their individual characters and came to sound like two modes only – the Ionian and Aeolian (see page 5). From these grew the major-minor key system upon which harmony was based for the next two centuries.

The 17th century also saw the invention of several new forms and designs, including opera, oratorio, fugue, the suite, sonata and concerto.

The violin family replaced the viols. And the orchestra gradually started to take shape, with a strong section of strings as its foundation – though the other sections were as yet not standardised.

All these experiments and changes prepared the musical ground for the two giants of later Baroque music: Bach and Handel.

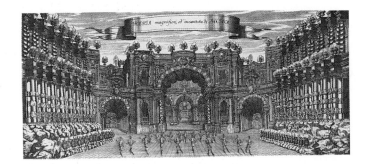

Stage sets for Baroque operas often aimed to suggest the massiveness and ornate decoration of Baroque architecture.

MONODY

Recitative

Basso continuo, or figured bass

In the Italian city of Florence during the last quarter of the 16th century, a group of composers and writers who called themselves the *Camerata* had come to believe that the elaborate weaving of the counterpoint in vocal music obscured the meaning of the words. The words, they felt, should always be more important than the music – and the music should portray the 'affection' (the mood or emotion) of the words. And so they began to experiment with a simpler style which they called **monody**: a single voice-line, supported by an instrumental bass-line upon which chords were constructed.

This voice-line rose and fell according to the meaning of the text and closely followed the natural speech-rhythms of the words. This style of writing for the voice – half singing, half reciting – came to be known as **recitative**. The accompaniment was extremely simple. All the composer wrote down beneath the melody was a bass-line to be played by a low string instrument, such as a cello. This was called the **basso continuo** since it 'continued' throughout the piece. But the composer expected another **continuo-player** on harpsichord, organ or lute to build up chords upon the bass-line to fill in the harmonies. As these chords had to be improvised, much depended upon the skill and musicianship of the player. Of course, the notes of the basso continuo provided clues, and composers often wrote figures below the notes to indicate what chords were expected. For this reason, such a bass-line is often called a **figured bass**. This idea of accompaniment provided by continuo instruments playing from a figured bass-line was to persist throughout the Baroque period, and provide the basis for the harmonies, and the texture, of almost every kind of music.

Assignment 28

At first, music written in the new monodic style was called *Le Nuove Musiche* (The New Music) – a name taken from the title of a collection of vocal pieces, published in 1602, by Giulio Caccini. Listen to one of the songs from Caccini's collection, called 'Amarilli':

1

A - ma - ril - li mia bel - la, Non cre-di-o del mio cor dol — ce de-si - o:

[smaller notes indicate the chords suggested by Caccini's figured bass-line]

1 Which instrument plays the basso continuo part in 'Amarilli'?
2 Which continuo instrument provides the chords?
3 Is the texture of this music homophonic or polyphonic?

THE EARLIEST OPERAS

In 1597, these new ideas were applied to a full-length music-drama – what we would call the first **opera**. This was *Dafne*, based, like many operas for the next two centuries, on an old Greek legend. The music was by Jacopo Peri, but unfortunately only a few fragments still survive. The first opera to come down to us complete is *Euridice*, with music by both Peri and Caccini.

Other operas were composed and the idea became extremely popular. These early operas included brief choruses, dances and instrumental pieces in simple chordal style, involving a small 'orchestra' consisting of a rather haphazard collection of instruments. The long stretches of recitative, however, tended to sound monotonous. If opera was to survive, a genius was needed to breathe life and excitement into the style. This was to be Claudio Monteverdi, whose life spans the late 16th and early 17th centuries.

'NEW STYLE' AND 'OLD STYLE'

The new monody, with its switch to melody accompanied by simple chords, was considered very modern and labelled **stile moderno**. However, a great deal of music (especially for the church) was still composed in contrapuntal style, now called **stile antico**. Some composers, including Monteverdi, cleverly drew on both styles.

Claudio Monteverdi (Italy; 1567–1643)

Monteverdi's *Orfeo*, composed in 1607, is the first truly great opera. His music very effectively heightens the dramatic impact of the story. He highlights powerful emotion in recitative passages by bringing leaps and chromatic intervals into the voice-line, while the accompaniment provides unexpected harmonies including frequent discords. There are short but dramatic choruses, and instrumental pieces in which Monteverdi boldly experiments with new combinations of tone-colours. He uses an orchestra of forty or so richly varied instruments (including violins, which are now beginning to take the place of viols – though, for some while, both play side by side).

Assignment 29

Find out about the story of Orfeo (Orpheus and Eurydice). Then listen to a scene from Monteverdi's opera, such as the second half of Act IV. This takes place in the underworld, and includes a chorus of Spirits and an **aria** (song) 'Qual onor' for Orfeo. In each verse, the melody is varied above an identically repeated bass. Notice how the rhythm of this bass-line continually causes the music to press steadily forward. (This kind of purposefully moving bass-line was to become one of the fingerprints of Baroque style.) Before each verse of this aria we hear an instrumental **ritornello** (meaning 'return').

After Orfeo's aria, there follow recitative passages as he risks a backward glance at Euridice – and, by doing so, loses her for ever.

1 Which instruments play the *ritornello* in Orfeo's aria?
2 Which *continuo* instruments are used in the recitative passages?
3 How does Monteverdi bring drama and emotion to the recitatives?
4 This scene ends with an orchestral *sinfonia* (meaning 'sounding together'). Identify some of the instruments included here.

Recitative and aria

Later 17th-century composers continued to use recitative as a means of swiftly telling the story, while giving greater importance to arias (songs) which portrayed the characters' thoughts and emotions as they were affected by events in the story. There were two kinds of recitative: **secco** (dry), supported by plain chords on continuo; and **stromentato** or **accompagnato** (accompanied), used when a composer felt that the dramatic nature of the words needed to be heightened by a simple orchestral accompaniment. The orchestra had pieces of its own to play, and sometimes there were choruses. While recitative took its rhythms from speech, arias and choruses often borrowed their rhythms from the dance.

The most popular Italian opera composer at the end of the 17th century was Alessandro Scarlatti. His operas often began with an **The Italian overture** overture in three sections: quick – slow – quick. This plan became known as the **Italian overture** and is important in that it was the seed from which the Classical symphony was to grow later on.

The 'da capo' aria Scarlatti designed the arias in his operas in **da capo** form – that is, in ternary form (ABA) but with only the first two sections written out. At the end of section B, the composer wrote *da capo* (or simply *D.C.*) meaning 'from the beginning'. In repeating the first section (A) the singer was expected to add his or her own vocal decorations to the printed melody.

In France, the leading opera composers were Lully and Rameau. Lully became court musician to Louis XIV, the 'Sun King'. His operas **The French overture** began with a **French overture**: a majestic, slow opening with crisp dotted rhythms, leading to a quicker section using imitation. This was sometimes followed by one or more dances, or perhaps a repeat of the slow opening section. French operas usually included *ballet*: spectacular dance sequences with lavish costumes and scenery in which the King himself often took part.

Baroque opera in England England was slow to take up opera. The one great English opera of the 17th century is *Dido and Aeneas* by Henry Purcell. This is a masterpiece in miniature. The high-point of the opera is Dido's recitative: 'Thy hand, Belinda', which leads into her deeply moving lament: 'When I am laid in earth . . . ' . For this, Purcell uses his favourite form – the ground bass.

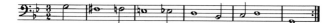

When Handel came to England in 1710, audiences had discovered a taste for Italian opera. He immediately took advantage of this and during the next few years composed thirty or more operas in Italian style. As an example of Baroque opera at its finest, listen to an **2** ⌨ aria from an opera by Handel, such as 'Piangerò' (I must weep) from *Giulio Cesare* or 'Dove sei' (Art thou troubled?) from *Rodelinda*.

Assignment 30 Listen again to Dido's Lament from Purcell's *Dido and Aeneas*, and to the aria from the opera by Handel. Note down all the differences – and also any similarities – you discover between these two pieces.

ORATORIO

Born at about the same time as opera was another important form of vocal music called **oratorio**. This took its name from St Philip Neri's Oratory ('hall of prayer') in Rome, where the first oratorios were performed. At first, oratorios were very similar to operas. They were made up of recitatives, arias and choruses, and acted out with scenery and costumes. The main difference was that an oratorio was based on a sacred story, usually taken from the Bible. In time, oratorios ceased to be acted, and were given musical presentation only, in churches and concert halls rather than theatres.

The main composers of oratorio in the 17th century were Carissimi (Italy; 1605-1674) and Schütz (Germany; 1585-1672). But the greatest oratorios of the Baroque period were composed during the first half of the 18th century, with words in English, by Handel. His finest are *Israel in Egypt*, *Samson* and – the most popular of all – *Messiah*. As in his operas, Handel uses recitative to move the story along, and arias for the more thoughtful, reflective moments. In some oratorios, he gives great weight and importance to choruses which vividly describe the more dramatic events in the story. An exciting example is the chorus from *Israel in Egypt*: 'He gave them hailstones for rain; fire mingled with blood ran along upon the ground'.

Assignment 31

Listen to the sequence of recitatives from *Messiah* which tell of the birth of Christ, beginning 'There were shepherds abiding in the field'. Describe Handel's accompaniment to these recitatives, and to the chorus which follows: 'Glory to God'.

Passion

Chorale

Bach composed *The Christmas Oratorio*, and also three settings of the *Passion* – a rather special type of oratorio telling the story of Christ's crucifixion. Besides recitatives, arias and choruses, Bach includes settings of **chorales** (German hymn-tunes) which he places at key points to intensify the most solemn and deeply-moving moments of the story.

2 💻 Assignment 32

From Bach's *Passion according to St Matthew*, listen to the section describing the last moments of the crucifixion. This includes the recitative: 'Ah, Golgotha!'; aria: 'See the Saviour's outstretched hands'; and chorale: 'If I should e'er forsake Thee'.

As you listen, discover and note down:
(a) two different types of recitative;
(b) the continuo instruments which accompany these recitatives;
(c) other instruments which Bach includes in his orchestra;
(d) two special ways in which Bach uses his chorus in this music;
(e) the difference in texture – and in musical and dramatic effect – of the chorale contrasted against the preceding music.

Cantata

Bach also composed more than 200 church cantatas (**cantata** meaning 'sung'). These are for soloists and chorus accompanied by orchestra and continuo, and are like miniature oratorios. A Bach cantata often opens with a weighty chorus, continues with recitatives, arias and duets for the soloists, then closes with a chorale. A fine example is No. 140, based upon the chorale *Wachet auf* ('Sleepers, wake').

INSTRUMENTAL MUSIC

During the Baroque period, instrumental music became, for the first time, equal in importance to vocal music. Composers still used some forms which had been popular during the Renaissance such as the canzona, ricercar, toccata, fantasia and variations (now including variation forms such as the chaconne and passacaglia). To these were added several new and important forms and designs, including the fugue, chorale prelude, suite, sonata and concerto.

Fugue

A **fugue** is a contrapuntal piece, essentially based upon the idea of imitation. It is usually written in three or four parts called 'voices' (whether, in fact, the fugue is vocal or instrumental) and these are referred to as soprano, alto, tenor or bass.

The detailed structure of a fugue can be rather complicated, but the basic idea is this. The entire piece grows mainly from a single fairly brief tune of strong musical character. The composer calls this tune the **subject** (in the sense of 'subject for discussion'). This subject is first heard in one voice only. Then it is imitated by the other voices in turn, each at its appropriate pitch:

Throughout the fugue, the subject enters in new keys - now in one voice, now another. These entries are separated by sections of music called episodes. A composer may base an episode on an idea taken from the subject itself, or he may use other musical material.

We can hear the origins of fugue in the imitative style of most Renaissance vocal music (see the music by Tallis on page 16) and in the instrumental canzona and ricercar. During the later Baroque, the idea was brought to perfection by Handel and, especially, Bach who composed many fine fugues for organ, a collection of *48 Preludes and Fugues* for harpsichord or clavichord, and *The Art of Fugue*.

Fugue means 'flight' - giving an idea of the voices fleeing away or chasing each other as they enter with the subject. Sometimes a composer writes in **fugal style** rather than writing a complete fugue.

Assignment 33

Listen to the complete recording of Bach's Fugue in C minor (No. 2 from the '48') and spot the number of times the subject enters.

Assignment 34

As an example of a vocal fugue, listen to the chorus: 'He trusted in God' from Handel's *Messiah*. In which order do the voices of the chorus enter with the fugue subject?

The chorale prelude

A popular type of piece for organ, particularly in Germany, was the **chorale prelude** based, as its name suggests, on a chorale melody. A composer might treat his chosen melody in fugal style, or write variations upon it, or weave one or more other melodic lines around it. Listen to Bach's chorale prelude: *Wachet auf*, which is in fact an arrangement of a movement from his cantata of the same name.

1 〔　〕 As the notes with brackets show, Bach takes a scrap of the chorale (music A) and from this builds a rhythmic tune (music B) which he weaves throughout the piece as a background to the chorale melody.

THE SUITE

Renaissance composers had sometimes linked dances together (as, for example, the pavan and galliard). Baroque composers extended this idea into the **suite**, a group of pieces for one or more instruments. Many suites were written for harpsichord, and eventually the most common plan brought together four dances from different countries:
1   a German **allemande**, 4/4 time, rather moderate in speed.
2   either a French **courante**, 3/2 or 6/4 time, moderately fast;
    or an Italian **corrente**, 3/4 or 3/8 time, rather quicker.
3   a Spanish **sarabande**, slow triple time, often with the second beat emphasised.
4   a lively **gigue** (English 'jig') usually in compound time.
However, before or after the gigue, a composer might introduce one or more dances such as the **minuet**, **bourrée**, **gavotte** or **passepied**. And sometimes a suite began with a **prelude** (or opening piece).

   The pieces in a suite were usually in the same key, and in **binary** form: two sections, A and B, each usually repeated. French composers such as Couperin, though, were fond of including pieces in the form of a **rondeau** (or **rondo**) in which a main theme alternated with contrasting episodes (**A B A C A** . . . .).

Suites were sometimes known by other names. Purcell called his suites 'lessons'; Couperin used the name 'ordre'; while Bach, though he composed six French Suites and six English Suites, sometimes used the name 'partita'.

A 'double-manual' harpsichord made in London in 1721.

·**1** 〔　〕 **Assignment 35**   Listen to the Sarabande and Gigue from Handel's Harpsichord Suite XI.
1   The basic plan of the Sarabande is binary form without repeats. How does Handel extend this to make it into a longer piece?
2   Is the form of the Gigue binary, ternary, rondo, or variations?

33

BAROQUE SONATAS

Sonata really means 'sounded', and therefore a piece to be played (as opposed to **cantata**, a piece to be sung). Many Baroque sonatas were for two violins and continuo (consisting, for example, of cello and harpsichord). Composers called these **trio sonatas** – trio meaning 'three' and referring to the three lines of music actually printed (the two violins and the figured bass-line) though, in fact, *four* players were needed. Sometimes one or both violins might be replaced by flute or oboe; and sometimes sonatas were written for a single melody instrument with continuo.

Sonata da camera

Sonata da chiesa

Baroque sonatas were of two main kinds: the **sonata da camera** or chamber sonata, intended for performance in the room of a home; and the **sonata da chiesa** or church sonata (in which continuo instruments were likely to be organ and perhaps bassoon). Both kinds of sonata commonly consisted of four movements, usually all in the same key, but contrasted in speed (slow : fast : slow : fast). Many movements were structured in binary form. Chamber sonatas were really suites, and so included dances; whereas church sonatas were more serious in character, with the quicker movements often written in fugal style.

The most important Baroque composers to write sonatas include Purcell, Corelli, Couperin, Bach and Handel.

A rather different kind of sonata is associated with Domenico Scarlatti, son of Alessandro Scarlatti, and born in the same year as Bach and Handel. He composed around 550 single-movement sonatas for solo harpsichord. These are very effectively written for the keyboard and include swift runs, leaps, quickly repeated notes, and sometimes tricky passages for crossed hands.

1 ▣ Assignment 36

Listen to the two movements from sonatas by Corelli and Couperin recorded on the cassette. As you listen to each piece, note down:
(a) the number, and kinds, of instruments involved;
(b) whether the music is likely to come from a *sonata da camera* or from a *sonata da chiesa*.

CONCERTO GROSSO

One of the most exciting types of Baroque music is the **concerto** (a word which may come from Italian, meaning 'get together'; or from Latin, meaning 'dispute'). We can trace the idea of the concerto back to the Renaissance. The seeds had been sown in the polychoral pieces written by composers such as Giovanni Gabrieli. The ideas of opposition and strong contrast led to the Baroque **concerto grosso.** In this, composers like Corelli, Handel and Bach (in his Brandenburg Concertos numbers 2, 4 and 5) contrasted two groups of instruments: a small group of soloists (often two violins and a cello) called the **concertino**, against an orchestra of strings called either the **ripieno** ('filling') or **tutti** ('all' or 'everyone'). A harpsichord or organ **continuo** filled out the texture when the ripieno group was playing, and continued to provide supporting harmonies on occasions when the concertino instruments played on their own.

Assignment 37

Listen to part of Corelli's 'Christmas' Concerto and then to the first movement of Bach's Brandenburg Concerto No. 2, identifying the instruments of (a) the *concertino* group, and (b) the *continuo*.

The solo concerto

From the concerto grosso grew the solo concerto, in which a single instrument was pitted against the weight of the string orchestra. The idea of contrast became stronger still, and the composer often gave the soloist some difficult and exciting passages to play. Solo concertos were most often in three movements, quick : slow : quick. The quick movements were built up in **ritornello** form. Ritornello means 'return' and refers to the main theme which was played by the orchestra at the beginning of the movement then returned, more or less complete, after each lightly accompanied **solo** section. Composers marked each ritornello section with the word **tutti** ('everyone') and so a plan of a movement in ritornello form might be written out as:

Tutti 1 : Solo 1 : Tutti 2 : Solo 2 : Tutti 3 (and so on).

2 ☐ **Assignment 38**

The Italian composer Antonio Vivaldi wrote more than 500 concertos (including both kinds: concerto grosso and solo concerto). Listen to the third movement of 'Autumn' from his set of four violin concertos called *The Four Seasons*. This third movement, called 'The Hunt' is in ritornello form. Here is the beginning of the ritornello theme:

Make a note of how many times this ritornello theme appears. Then afterwards, make out a plan to show how Vivaldi builds up this music.

THE ORCHESTRA

It was during the Baroque period that the orchestra first began to take shape. At first, 'orchestra' tended to describe a haphazard collection of whatever instruments were at hand. But as the 17th century progressed, the perfecting of string instruments (the violin in particular) by superb craftsmen such as the Amati, Guarneri and Stradivari families led to the establishing of the string section as a self-contained unit. This became the basis of the orchestra – a central nucleus to which composers would add other instruments in ones and twos as occasion offered: flutes (or recorders), oboes, bassoons, perhaps horns, and occasionally trumpets and kettle drums.

One constant feature of the Baroque orchestra, however, was the harpsichord or organ **continuo**, filling out the harmonies, decorating the textures and, in fact, holding the ensemble together.

A strong characteristic of Baroque orchestral music is **contrast**, especially of dynamics (loud/soft) and of instrumental timbres. A Baroque composer often contrasts bright ribbons of sound, such as two oboes or two trumpets, against a background of strings. Or he may contrast 'blocks' of sound of different colours – for example: a passage for strings, then for wind, then for both combined. Often, you will notice what have been called 'terraced dynamics' – sudden changes in volume level such as *forte*, a drop to *piano*, and then an abrupt return to *forte*. Sometimes, the quiet phrase may be a repeat of the preceding loud phrase, so creating an echo effect.

Assignment 39

Listen to movements from Bach's Orchestral Suite No. 3, noting down any characteristic sounds of the Baroque orchestra that you hear.

The main characteristics of Baroque music

1. At first, a switch to a lighter, homophonic texture: melody supported by simple chords; but polyphonic textures soon return.
2. The basso continuo, or figured bass, becomes the foundation for most types of Baroque music – providing a purposeful bass-line which causes the music to press steadily forward from beginning to end.
3. One 'affection' or mood usually persists throughout an entire piece.
4. Viols gradually replaced by the violin family; the string section becomes the basis of the Baroque orchestra, always with keyboard continuo (harpsichord or organ) filling out the harmonies above the figured bass and decorating the textures.
5. By the end of the 17th century, the system of modes replaced by the major-minor key system.
6. Main forms used: binary, ternary (*da capo* aria), rondeau, variations (including ground bass, chaconne, passacaglia), ritornello, fugue.
7. Main types of music: chorale, recitative and aria, opera, oratorio, cantata; Italian overture, French overture, toccata, prelude, chorale prelude, dance suite, sonata da camera, sonata da chiesa, concerto grosso, solo concerto.
8. Often, an exuberance in the music: energetic rhythms drive the music forward; melodies often spun out into long, flowing lines with many ornaments (such as trills); contrasts (especially in concertos) of instrumental timbres, of few instruments against many, and of loud against soft ('terraced dynamics', sometimes echo effects).

Assignments

40 *Research* Find out more about the life and music of each of these Baroque composers, writing a brief report on each one:
Monteverdi; Purcell; Bach; Handel.

1 ⊡ 41 Listen to the five extracts of Baroque music recorded on the cassette. Describe each extract in as much detail as you can, mentioning:
(a) the instruments and/or voices that are used;
(b) the rhythm and texture of the music;
(c) the type of piece (also suggesting a likely composer).

42 Explain the meaning of:
basso continuo; recitative; ritornello; *da capo* aria; trio sonata.

43 Describe the differences between:
(a) a French overture and an Italian overture
(b) a sonata da camera and a sonata da chiesa
(c) a concerto grosso and a solo concerto

44 Listen to: (a) the *Gloria* from a mass by William Byrd, followed by the *Gloria* from Bach's Mass in B minor;
or: (b) a motet by Palestrina, and then an anthem by Purcell.
Note down any fingerprints of style you hear which give each piece the special flavour of its particular period, Renaissance or Baroque.

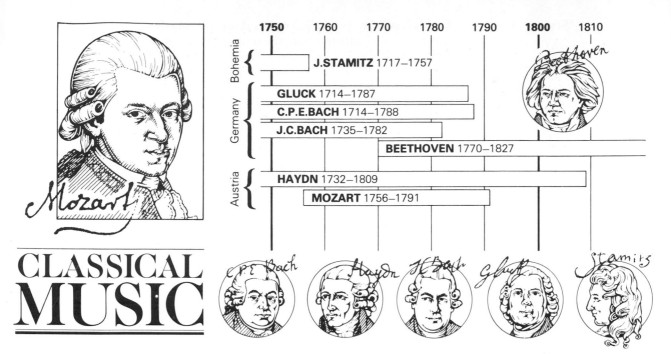

CLASSICAL MUSIC

'Classical' and 'classic' both come from the Latin word *classicus*, meaning a citizen (and, later on, a writer) of the highest class. And so we have come to use these words in connection with anything we consider to be top class, first rate, of lasting value. We count the plays of Shakespeare or the novels of Charles Dickens among the 'classics' of literature; and we describe the style of architecture of ancient Greece and Rome as 'classical' – meaning a style which places an importance on grace and simplicity, beauty of line and shape, balance and proportion, order and control.

As far as music is concerned, the word 'classical' may be used in two different ways. People sometimes speak in a very general way of 'classical music' when they think of all music as being divided into two very broad categories: 'classical' and 'pop'. To a musician, though, 'Classical' with a capital 'C' has a special, very much more precise, meaning. It refers specifically to music composed between 1750 and 1810 – a fairly brief period which includes the music of Haydn and Mozart, and the earlier compositions of Beethoven.

These two dates, 1750 and 1810, should not be applied too strictly however. Baroque style did not make an abrupt change to Classical style. There were signs of change as far back as the 1730s and so Classical style, in fact, began to grow up within the last years of the Baroque period. The Baroque trio sonata began to give way to the Classical sonata; and the Italian overture, found in many Baroque operas, grew into the Classical symphony. While Bach continued to compose in the mainly contrapuntal style of the late Baroque, his sons – though they held great respect for their father's music – favoured a lighter, more homophonic style in their own compositions.

As for a date fixing the close of the Classical period, some might suggest 1827 (the year of the death of Beethoven) while others would offer a much earlier date – for instance, 1800.

'Style galant'	Early Classical style is called **style galant** – a 'courtly style' which aimed chiefly to please the listener. Much of this music is lacking in depth, but at its finest – in the music of Bach's sons, Carl Philip Emanuel and Johann Christian, and the early compositions of Haydn and Mozart – it is polished, polite and extremely elegant.
Later Classical style	Later, as Classical style matured, it came to emphasise more and more the qualities we associate with Classical architecture: grace and beauty of line (melody) and shape (the form or design used by a composer to build up his music), proportion and balance, moderation and control. In particular, the Classical composer strikes a perfect balance in his music between expressiveness and formal structure.
Texture	Baroque music had been mainly *polyphonic*, with the strands of counterpoint woven into an intricate texture, often with harpsichord continuo sounding in the background. The texture of music in the Classical period tends to be lighter, clearer, less complicated, and – though counterpoint was by no means forgotten – basically *homophonic*: tunes above a chordal accompaniment.
1 ▣ Assignment 45	Notice these main 'fingerprints' of Classical style as you listen to the opening of Haydn's String Quartet, Opus 64 No. 5 ('The Lark'). (This is an example of *chamber music* – music intended to be played in a room, rather than a large hall, by a small group of solo musicians. A string quartet is for two violins, viola and cello.)
THE ORCHESTRA	The orchestra, which had begun to take shape during the Baroque period, now started to grow. Harpsichord continuo was still included at first, mainly as a means of knitting the texture together. In time, though, the continuo fell out of use and composers began to use wind instruments, especially the horns, to bind the texture.

In the earlier part of the Classical period, orchestras were still small and variable: a basis of strings, to which were usually added two horns and one or two flutes or a pair of oboes. Soon, however, composers were including both flutes and oboes, one or two bassoons, and occasionally two trumpets and a pair of kettle drums. Clarinets found a regular place towards the end of the 18th century, then making the woodwind a self-contained section of the orchestra.

The orchestra at the end of the 18th century included:

1 or 2 flutes
2 oboes
2 clarinets
2 bassoons
2 horns
2 trumpets
2 kettle drums
strings

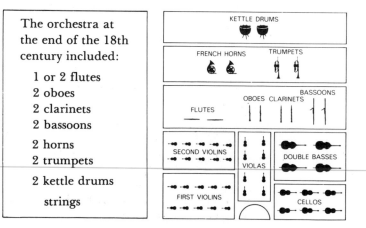

Assignment 46

In order to compare the use of the orchestra in the Baroque and Classical periods, and to hear and pick out the main differences between Baroque and Classical styles, listen to the first four minutes or so of each of these pieces:

  Baroque: Orchestral Suite No. 3 in D by Bach (1685-1750)
  Classical: Symphony No. 100 ('The Military') by Haydn (1732-1809)

(a)   Which style, Baroque or Classical, is mainly polyphonic, and which is mainly homophonic (tune with accompaniment)?

(b)   Which style has a lighter, clearer texture, and which has a more complicated texture backed by harpsichord continuo?

(c)   Which of these two styles, do you think, makes use of a richer variety of tunes, rhythms, dynamics, with frequent changes of mood and timbre (instrumental 'colour')?

(d)   What are the main differences between these two orchestras, and the ways in which their composers use them?

MUSIC FOR PIANO

During the Classical period, for the first time in musical history, music for instruments became more important than music for voices. Many works were written for, or included, the pianoforte – usually called 'piano' for short. This had been invented as early as 1698 by Bartolomeo Cristofori in Italy. By 1700 he had built at least one instrument of this kind. He called it **gravicembalo col piano e forte** – 'a harpsichord with soft and loud'. But whereas in a harpsichord the strings were plucked, in Cristofori's instrument they were struck by hammers – lightly, or more forcefully, according to the amount of pressure made by the player's fingers upon the keys.

This was to give the piano considerable powers of expression, and offer exciting possibilities. Not only might a pianist make sudden contrasts between soft and loud, he could also control all the various shades of tone and volume in between. Sounds could be made to grow gradually louder, or gradually softer, and further contrasts might be made between **legato** (smooth and sustained) and **staccato** (crisp and detached). A player might shape an expressive melody in **cantabile** ('singing') style with the right hand against a quieter accompaniment with the left hand.

Alberti bass

A favourite kind of accompaniment pattern often used by Classical composers became known as the 'Alberti bass'. This consisted of simple broken chords repeated in the left hand, keeping the music moving while outlining harmonies to support the melody.

At first, the piano was rather slow to make ground, no doubt due to the crudeness of the early models. But by the 1760s, C.P.E. Bach, whose keyboard music made considerable impact upon Haydn, accepted the piano as being on equal terms with the harpsichord and the clavichord. And at about the same time, J.C. Bach, whose music greatly influenced the young Mozart, gave the first public performances of music on the piano in London. For quite a while, keyboard music was printed with the heading 'for pianoforte or harpsichord', but by the end of the 18th century the harpsichord had fallen out of use and the piano had completely taken its place.

1 ⊡ **Assignment 47**   Listen to the beginning of Mozart's Sonata in F major (K332):

In what ways, do you think, is this music more suited to the piano than to the harpsichord?

SONATAS   Sonata (meaning 'sounded') was the name a Classical composer gave to a work in several movements for one or two instruments only – for instance: piano, or violin and piano. If three instruments took part he called his work a trio; if four, he called it a quartet; five made it a quintet; and so on. Other important types of composition, for orchestra, were the symphony and the concerto.

THE SYMPHONY   The **symphony** (meaning 'sounding together') was in fact a sonata for orchestra. It grew from the Italian overture (often called **sinfonia**) which had three sections, contrasted in speed: quick – slow – quick. In the early Classical symphony these became three separate movements; later, the usual number became four, with the minuet and trio (a dance borrowed from the Baroque suite) inserted between the slow movement and the brisk finale. Many composers took a hand in shaping the symphony – including the Italian composer Sammartini, Johann Stamitz who became director of one of the most famous orchestras in the mid 18th century at the German court of Mannheim, and C.P.E. and J.C. Bach. But it was Haydn and Mozart who enriched and perfected the symphony during the second half of the 18th century.

The movements of a Classical symphony, well contrasted in speed and character, are usually set out according to this basic plan:

> **First movement**   at a fairly fast speed; usually built up in what is known as 'sonata form' (which is described opposite).
> **Second movement**   at a slower speed, and more song-like; often in ternary form (ABA), or variations, or perhaps sonata form again.
> **Third movement**   at this point, Haydn and Mozart wrote a minuet and trio; Beethoven later transformed this into the much brisker and more vigorous *scherzo* (meaning 'a joke').
> **Fourth movement (Finale)**   at a fast speed, and often light-hearted in mood; in rondo form (ABACA . . .), or sonata form, or perhaps in a mixture of both; sometimes, variations.

Assignment 48   Listen to a symphony by Haydn, such as No. 94 in G ('The Surprise'), No. 103 in E flat ('The Drumroll'), or his last symphony, No. 104 in D ('The London').
(a)   Describe the orchestra which Haydn uses.
(b)   How do the four movements of the Symphony contrast with each other in speed and character?
(c)   Note down some of the ways in which Haydn achieves variety and contrast *within* each movement.

Works such as trios and quartets were also in four movements, planned in exactly the same way as symphonies. Sonatas might have four, or sometimes three, movements. The Classical concerto, which developed from the Baroque solo concerto, did not include the minuet, and so the number of movements was always three.

SONATA FORM   In each of these various kinds of composition, the first movement is almost always designed in what is called **sonata form**. This name is rather misleading. 'Sonata form' does not refer to the structure of a complete work, but to a special kind of musical form or design used to build up a single movement of a work – including symphonies, quartets, and so on, as well as sonatas.

Baroque composers had tended to write melodies in long-flowing lines. The length of a piece of music often depended upon the spinning-out of these melodies, with the same 'affection' (or mood), and the same rhythm, generally persisting throughout. The melodies of Classical composers tend to be shorter, with clear-cut outlines and incisive rhythms. Contrasting tunes and rhythms closely follow one another, so that the mood is constantly changing, emphasised by frequent changes of timbre (instrumental 'colour'). When Classical composers looked for a means of building up these varying elements into a balanced, coherent musical design, they eventually found that sonata form provided the most satisfying solution.

Sonata form actually grew out of binary (two-part) form – yet it is ternary (three-part) in outline in that it consists of three main sections, called **exposition**, **development**, and **recapitulation**. (There may be a slow introduction before the sonata form really begins.)

1   Exposition   Here, the composer 'exposes', or states, his musical material. He calls his main ideas **subjects** (meaning 'subjects for later discussion'). There are two subjects – each of which may be made up of several musical ideas rather than a single melody. These two subjects are contrasted in key, and usually also in character.
The **first subject** (or group of ideas) is in the tonic, the 'home' key, and is most often vigorous and rhythmic. This is followed by a bridge passage which modulates, or changes key, and leads to:
The **second subject** (or group of ideas) in a new, but related, key – often the dominant, or the relative major if the tonic is a minor key. The second subject is usually more tuneful, less vigorous, than the first. (Composers often mark the exposition to be repeated so the listener may have a second chance to fix these ideas in mind.)

41

2 Development

In this section the composer 'develops' or explores the musical possibilities of ideas presented in the exposition. Any aspect of the two subjects (or the bridge passage) may be brought under musical discussion. The composer may seize upon a rhythmic or tuneful fragment and repeat it while taking the music through a variety of different keys (but avoiding the tonic key). Fragments of different ideas may be combined, or set into opposition one against another. A strong feeling of tension, of dramatic conflict, may be built up, reaching a climax when the music purposefully makes for 'home' – the tonic key – and the beginning of the recapitulation.

3 Recapitulation

The composer now 'recapitulates', or repeats in a slightly different form, the music of the exposition section. The first subject is heard in the tonic key as before. The bridge passage is altered so that the second subject *also* now appears in the tonic.

The composer then rounds off the movement with a **coda.**

This diagram shows a basic plan for a piece built up in sonata form:

Exposition (presentation)			Development (discussion)	Recapitulation (restatement)			Coda
First subject (tonic)	Bridge (changing key)	Second subject (in a new key)	– moving through new keys, discussing, developing, combining and opposing ideas from the exposition	First subject (tonic)	Bridge (now altered)	Second subject (tonic)	to round off

Assignment 49

The first movement of Mozart's *Eine Kleine Nachtmusik* ('A Little Night Music') is designed in sonata form. Mozart also calls this a serenade (evening music) which, like the divertimento (music to divert, or entertain) was of a lighter character than a symphony and often intended for performance in the open air.

Listen to this music, then answer these questions:

1 How does the second subject contrast with the first subject?
2 In which key does the second subject appear:
   (a) in the exposition, and (b) in the recapitulation?
3 Which musical ideas, first heard in the exposition, does Mozart use to build up the development section?
4 With which musical ideas does he build up the coda?
5 Describe the orchestra which plays this 'night music'.

Vienna, the capital city of Austria, became the most important musical centre during the Classical period. In this city, at various times, lived Gluck, Haydn, Mozart, Beethoven and Schubert.

THE CONCERTO

The Classical concerto, featuring a solo instrument in competition with the orchestra, grew from the Baroque solo concerto. Its three movements (fairly fast : slow : fast) correspond to the movements of the symphony, but without the minuet. The first movement, though, is in a modified sonata form, which begins with a 'double exposition': one exposition for the orchestra alone, presenting the main musical material all in the tonic key; followed by the entry of the soloist and a second exposition, now with the second subject group in the related key. A composer often holds back one or more themes from the first exposition in order to add interest and variety when these are introduced during the second.

Then follows the development section and recapitulation, shared by soloist and orchestra. Towards the end of the recapitulation, the orchestra pauses, and the soloist plays a **cadenza** – a showy passage based on themes heard earlier, which displays the brilliance of the player's technique. (Originally, a soloist was expected to improvise a cadenza on the spot; later on, composers began to write out the music they expected to be played.) A cadenza usually ends with a trill – the signal for the orchestra to re-enter to play the coda.

Assignment 50

Listen to the first movement of a concerto by Mozart – for example, Piano Concerto No. 23 in A, or Horn Concerto No. 3 in E flat.

Listen for, and notice:

(a) the effect made by the 'delayed appearance' of the soloist;

(b) the variety of musical material shared by soloist and orchestra;

(c) the contrast between passages where the soloist is heard alone or quietly accompanied by the orchestra, and loud orchestral **tutti** passages (**tutti** meaning 'everyone');

(d) sections of musical dialogue between soloist and orchestra;

(e) the musical and dramatic effect of the soloist's cadenza (based on the themes of the movement) followed by the orchestral coda.

OPERA

Although Classical composers wrote a great deal for the church, in vocal music it was opera that attracted most interest. The two greatest opera composers of the period were Gluck and Mozart.

Gluck (1714-1787)

Gluck was one of several composers (and critics) who were concerned that opera was becoming too stilted, too stereotyped. Singers had taken on such importance that the music was often composed to suit them rather than the story, with the result that the action was frequently held up while singers were allowed to show off their technical brilliance. Gluck decided it was time for this to change.

He first put his ideas into practice on *Orfeo ed Euridice*, his best-known opera which was performed in Vienna in 1762. (This made use of the same Greek legend as Monteverdi's *Orfeo*, composed in 1607.) Then, five years later, in a printed preface to his opera *Alceste*, Gluck explained his ideas of what an opera should be. The music should serve the story while still reflecting the drama and emotion of the poetry. There should be less distinction between aria and recitative, and the action should be more continuous, avoiding interruptions merely for vocal display at the demands of the singers. Instruments should be chosen and used to suit each situation in the story, and the overture should prepare the audience for the nature of the drama which was to follow.

2 ▣ Assignment 51

From Gluck's opera *Orfeo ed Euridice*, listen to Orfeo's aria: 'Che farò' (usually translated: 'What is life to me without thee?').

What qualities are there in this aria – both in the melody and in the orchestral accompaniment – which identify the music as being Classical in style rather than Baroque?

Mozart (1756-1791)

It has been suggested that, whereas Gluck reformed opera, Mozart transformed it – by his musical genius and dramatic instinct. His three greatest operas are *The Marriage of Figaro*, *Don Giovanni*, and *The Magic Flute* (which is a **Singspiel**, a type of opera in which singing is interspersed with spoken dialogue). These operas show Mozart's keen observation of human nature which enables him to bring life and warmth to his characters. Arias, while deepening our understanding of a character, often help to carry the story forward.

Mozart makes the final scene of an act into an elaborate structure during which all the characters join in an **ensemble** ('together') – everyone singing at once, but with each character voicing his or her own reaction to the situation which has come about.

The orchestra in a Mozart opera plays an important part in the unfolding of the story, mirroring the mood and drama of the action and adding interesting detail; but always enhancing, rather than diminishing, the importance of the voices.

2 ▣ Assignment 52

Find out about the story of Mozart's **opera buffa** ('comic opera') *Don Giovanni*. Then listen to Leporello's 'Catalogue' aria in which he gives an account of his master's many previous loves.

(a) Which type of voice sings this aria?

(b) How does Mozart bring a light-hearted, joking mood to this aria?

Ludwig van Beethoven (1770–1827)

Beethoven is a massive figure in the history of music. Like Monteverdi, two centuries earlier, he strides across two eras. He has been described as the last of the Classical composers and, at the same time, the first of the Romantics. Unlike most composers before him, Beethoven did not write music to please a wealthy patron. He composed in order to please himself.

It is usual to divide Beethoven's life and work into three periods. The first, showing the influence of Haydn and Mozart, includes the first two symphonies, the first three piano concertos, the first six string quartets and the first dozen or so of his 32 piano sonatas. By the time Beethoven had written these works he was turned thirty, and had already noticed the signs of approaching deafness.

The works of the second period are written in a more individual, personal style – on a grander scale, and with greater depths of feeling. To this middle period belong the Third to Eighth Symphonies, the Fourth and Fifth Piano Concertos and the Violin Concerto, the three 'Razumovsky' String Quartets, the 'Moonlight', 'Waldstein' and 'Appassionata' Piano Sonatas, and Beethoven's only opera, *Fidelio*.

To the third period belong the Ninth Symphony ('Choral'), the Mass in D, and the last string quartets and sonatas. During this last period Beethoven's deafness became total, completely cutting him off from the world of sound except in his imagination.

Taking Classical forms used by Haydn and Mozart, Beethoven modified and expanded them. His works tend to be weightier, on a much larger scale. In the development section of a sonata form movement he makes a more searching exploration of ideas chosen for discussion. He gives the coda greater importance, sometimes continuing to explore material in such a way that it amounts to a second development section. Slow movements portray a deeper emotional intensity; the minuet becomes transformed into the brisk and vigorous scherzo; and more weight and importance is given to a final movement to balance the first.

Drama and conflict are essential ingredients in Beethoven's style, stemming from a powerful, often violent, rhythmic drive, a sharper use of discords, frequently marked *sforzando* (forcing the tone), and striking contrasts – of timbres (tone-colours), pitches (high against low) and dynamics (loud against soft). During a *crescendo*, when the loudest chord is expected, Beethoven will often take the listener by surprise by making a sudden drop to *piano*.

Beethoven increased the size of the orchestra. To that used by Haydn in his last symphonies (see page 38) he adds a third horn in the Third Symphony ('Eroica') and piccolo, double bassoon and three trombones in the Finale of the Fifth Symphony. These instruments are used again in the Ninth Symphony ('Choral') which also includes solo voices and mixed chorus. Bass drum, cymbals and triangle are added to the percussion, and the number of horns is increased to four.

Assignment 53

Listen to a work by Beethoven, such as his 'Appassionata' Piano Sonata (No. 23 in F minor) or his Third or Fifth Symphony. Compare this music with a work you have listened to by Haydn or Mozart, pointing out some of the differences in style and impact.

The main characteristics of Classical music

1 Lighter, clearer texture than Baroque, less complicated; mainly homophonic - melody above chordal accompaniment (but counterpoint by no means forgotten).

2 An emphasis on grace and beauty of melody and form, proportion and balance, moderation and control; polished and elegant in character with expressiveness and formal structure held in perfect balance.

3 More variety and contrast within a piece: of keys, tunes, rhythms and dynamics (now using *crescendo* and *sforzando*); frequent changes of mood and timbre.

4 Melodies tend to be shorter than those of Baroque, with clear-cut phrases and clearly marked cadences.

5 Orchestra increases in size and range; harpsichord continuo falls out of use; woodwind becomes a self-contained section.

6 Harpsichord replaced by the piano: early piano music thinnish in texture, often with 'Alberti bass' accompaniment (Haydn and Mozart) but later becoming richer, more sonorous and powerful (Beethoven).

7 Importance given to instrumental music - main kinds: sonata, trio, string quartet, symphony, concerto, serenade, divertimento.

8 Sonata form the most important design - used to build up the first movement of most large-scale works, but also other movements, and single pieces (such as overtures).

Assignments

54 *Research* Find out more about the life and music of each of these Classical composers, writing a brief report on each one:
Haydn; Mozart; Beethoven.

2 ▱ 55 Listen to the third movement from Mozart's last symphony: No. 41 in C major (nicknamed 'The Jupiter').
(a) What name is given to this type of movement in a symphony?
(b) Which 'fingerprints' of style do you hear which indicate that this music was composed during the Classical period?

56 Write a brief description of each of the following:
string quartet; first subject; *cadenza*; 'Alberti bass'; *sforzando*.

57 During the Classical period, what differences would an audience expect to hear between the first movement of a symphony and the first movement of a concerto?

58 A Arrange these composers in the order in which they were born:
Handel; Mozart; Purcell; Pérotin; Giovanni Gabrieli.
B To which musical period does each composer belong?

59 Of the four periods: Medieval, Renaissance, Baroque and Classical, which music has interested you the most? What are the reasons for your choice?

Special Assignment B

In the two boxes below you will find various kinds of music belonging to either the Baroque or the Classical period. As before, your assignment here is to listen to a varied programme made up of extracts taken from some of these pieces – selected from both lists, but arranged into a mixed order. As you listen, identify the style – Baroque or Classical – of each item, and also the kind of piece being performed.

Baroque (1600-1750)	Classical (1750-1810)
* a scene from an opera by Monteverdi	* a piano sonata by Haydn
* a dance from a keyboard suite by Purcell	* a string quartet by Haydn
* a chorus from an oratorio by Handel	* the third movement from a concerto by Mozart
* a trio sonata by Corelli	* the finale from a symphony by Haydn
* a keyboard fugue by Bach	* a scene from an opera by Mozart
* the first movement from a concerto by Vivaldi	* the scherzo from a violin sonata by Beethoven
* a piece from Handel's Suite: 'The Water Music'	* a movement from Beethoven's Third Symphony ('Eroica')

Before listening: Refresh your memory about the main pointers to Baroque and Classical styles by reading the checklists on pages 36 and 47.

As you listen: Make a note of all the 'fingerprints' of style you discover in each piece – together with any other interesting details about the music.

After listening: Organise your findings by writing a brief report on each piece of music, mentioning:
1 The musical period – Baroque or Classical – during which it was composed.
2 The type of piece, with details of the forces needed to perform the music.
3 All the other 'clues' you discovered while listening to the music which helped you to make your identification.

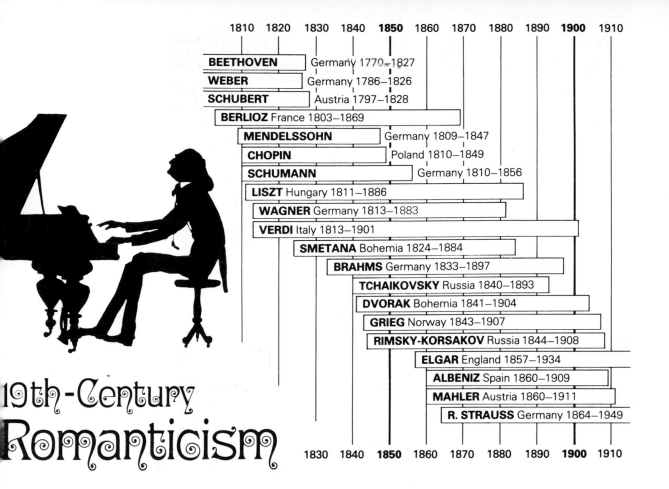

	1810	1820	1830	1840	**1850**	1860	1870	1880	1890	**1900**	1910

BEETHOVEN Germany 1770–1827
WEBER Germany 1786–1826
SCHUBERT Austria 1797–1828
BERLIOZ France 1803–1869
MENDELSSOHN Germany 1809–1847
CHOPIN Poland 1810–1849
SCHUMANN Germany 1810–1856
LISZT Hungary 1811–1886
WAGNER Germany 1813–1883
VERDI Italy 1813–1901
SMETANA Bohemia 1824–1884
BRAHMS Germany 1833–1897
TCHAIKOVSKY Russia 1840–1893
DVORAK Bohemia 1841–1904
GRIEG Norway 1843–1907
RIMSKY-KORSAKOV Russia 1844–1908
ELGAR England 1857–1934
ALBENIZ Spain 1860–1909
MAHLER Austria 1860–1911
R. STRAUSS Germany 1864–1949

1830	1840	**1850**	1860	1870	1880	1890	**1900**	1910

19th-Century Romanticism

The word **Romanticism** was first used to describe the stirrings of new ideas in painting and literature towards the end of the 18th century. This word was later taken up by musicians to describe the changes in musical style which took place soon after the turn of the century.

Classical composers had aimed to strike a balance in their music between expressiveness and formal structure. Romantic composers shifted this balance. They looked for a greater freedom of form and design in their music, and a more powerful and intense expression of emotion, often revealing their innermost thoughts and feelings, even sufferings. We find emotion to some degree, of course, in almost all music, whatever the style or period may be, but we find it expressed most strongly of all in the music of the Romantic period.

Many Romantic composers read widely and took a keen interest in art, forming close friendships with writers and painters. Often, the inspiration behind a composition by a Romantic composer was sparked off by a painting which he had seen, or by a book or a poem he had read. Imagination, fantasy and a quest for adventure are important ingredients in Romantic style. Among the many ideas which hold a strong fascination for Romantic composers are: far-off lands and the distant past; dreams, night and moonlight; rivers, lakes and forests; nature and the seasons; the joy and pain of love (especially young love); legends and fairy-tales; mystery, magic and the supernatural.

An impression of the Wolf's Glen scene by Moritz von Schwind.

2 ⊡ **Assignment 60**

Several of these ingredients can be found in the first important Romantic opera: *Der Freischütz* ('The Magic Marksman') by Weber. This is based on a German ghost story, telling of a hunter who acquires seven magic bullets. The first six strike wherever he directs; but the seventh, wherever the Devil directs.

Find out more about the story of this opera. Then listen to the Wolf's Glen Scene which ends Act 2. Even without benefit of setting and stage action, Weber's music conjures up a vivid impression of the sinister, terrifying atmosphere of the haunted Wolf's Glen. In what ways does Weber use both orchestra and voices to achieve this?

THE ORCHESTRA

During the Romantic period, we find composers widening the range of their musical materials. Melodies, whether tender or passionate, become more lyrical and song-like with swifter, more adventurous modulations. Harmonies become richer and intensely emotional with a more powerful use of discords, bringing in chromatic notes from outside the key (chromatic is from a Greek word meaning 'coloured').

There was an enormous increase in both the size and range of the orchestra. The brass section, soon completed by the addition of the tuba, now took on far greater importance as its range and flexibility were increased by the invention of the valve system. Composers now sometimes wrote for woodwind instruments in threes or even fours, adding piccolo, cor anglais, bass clarinet and double bassoon. The choice of percussion instruments became more varied and colourful, and it became necessary to increase the number of string-players in order to maintain a balance of sound between the four sections.

Romantic composers revelled in exploring this wider range of pitch and volume, richer harmonies, and new possibilities of combining and contrasting instrumental timbres. Their music offers a rich variety of types of composition – ranging from works requiring just one or a few performers, such as piano pieces, songs and chamber music (trios, quartets, and so on) to spectacular musical canvasses involving a huge number of performers, such as the operas of Wagner or the lengthy orchestral works of Berlioz, Mahler and Richard Strauss.

THE GERMAN *LIED*

There was a rich flowering of songs during the Romantic period, especially the German **Lied** for solo voice and piano (the plural is **Lieder** – 'songs'). There are two main kinds of Lied. In the first, which is called **strophic**, the same music is basically repeated for each verse of the poem. In the second kind, which the Germans call **durchkomponiert**, 'through-composed', different music is composed to each verse thoughout the song. In a through-composed song, of course, a composer can more faithfully match the voice-part to the changing moods and dramatic events of the poem, and also mirror these in some detail in the piano-part. An important aspect of most lieder is that the piano accompaniment is far more than a mere 'prop' for the voice. Instead, voice and piano are brought together in equal partnership.

The first great Romantic composer of Lieder was Schubert, who in his brief lifetime, composed more than 600 songs, touching on every possible mood and emotion. Among the best known are the powerfully dramatic *Erlkönig* (The Erlking) composed when he was 18, *An die Musik* (To Music), *Die Forelle* (The Trout), *An Sylvia* (To Sylvia), and *Ständchen* (Serenade). Other important Lieder composers were Schumann, Brahms, and later, Hugo Wolf and Richard Strauss.

Occasionally, a composer might set a whole group of poems linked to the same idea, perhaps even sketching a story. A sequence of songs linked together in this way in called a 'song cycle'. Fine examples are Schubert's *Winterreise* (Winter Journey) and Schumann's *Frauenliebe und Leben* (Woman's Love and Life).

Assignment 61

Listen to a short programme of German Lieder. First, discover what each song is about. Then as you listen, make a note of:
(a) ways in which the voice-part brings out the meaning of the poem;
(b) ways in which the piano-part helps to create the special mood or atmosphere of the song;
(c) whether the structure of the song is strophic or through-composed.

MUSIC FOR PIANO

Several improvements were made to the piano during the 19th century. The number of notes was increased, felt was used instead of leather to cover the hammers, and the frame was made of metal instead of wood, allowing greater tension on the strings which were now longer and thicker. All this gave the piano a rounder, richer sound and a wider range in pitch, volume and tone. Romantic composers began to explore the full range of the keyboard, building up rich and varied textures which relied on a much greater use of the sustaining pedal.

Almost all Romantic composers wrote music for piano, but among the most important were Schubert, Mendelssohn, Chopin, Schumann, Liszt and Brahms. Although they sometimes wrote sonatas they more often chose to express themselves in fairly short, individual pieces. There was a great variety of these, including dances such as the waltz, mazurka and polonaise, and 'mood' or 'character' pieces such as the impromptu (meaning 'on the spur of the moment'), romance, song without words, prelude, nocturne (night-piece), ballade, intermezzo ('interlude') and rhapsody. Many pieces presented two contrasting moods and were often designed in ternary form (ABA).

Another type of piece was the *étude*, or study, which was intended to improve some aspect of a player's technique. There was, in fact, a great advancement in technique at this time, giving rise to the 'virtuoso' – meaning a musician of extraordinary technical skill. The two most famous examples were the violinist, Paganini, and the composer-pianist, Franz Liszt. Although Liszt wrote many thoughtful and poetic compositions he was known more for his brilliant display pieces which he performed to amazed and delighted audiences.

The composer who showed the deepest understanding of the piano's character and capabilities, however, was Fryderyk Chopin. He had a gift for writing inspired melodies which he often harmonised in an unusual way. Typical of Chopin's style is an expressive melody made to sing out above a fairly straightforward accompaniment, relying on careful use of the sustaining pedal. But although Chopin's music can be dreamy and poetic, as in his Nocturnes, it can also be fiery and dramatic, as in his Polonaises and in many of his Etudes.

Assignment 62

Listen to two Romantic piano pieces – perhaps one by Chopin, another by Liszt.
1 Describe the mood created at the beginning of each piece, and any changes of mood later on.
2 Which piece did you find most interesting to listen to? Why?
3 What differences are there, in sound and style, between these two Romantic piano pieces and a Classical sonata by Haydn or Mozart?

PROGRAMME MUSIC

The closer links formed during the Romantic period between music and literature and painting led to a much keener interest in composing **programme music** – music which 'tells a story' or is in some way descriptive and so conjures up pictures in the mind of the listener. (Music without such a background, but which is intended to be enjoyed purely for its own sake, is called **absolute music.**)

Many piano pieces written by Romantic composers are programmatic in character, but it was in orchestral music that composers were able to express these ideas most vividly. There are three main types of programme music for orchestra: the programme symphony, the concert overture, and the symphonic poem (also called the tone poem).

The programme symphony

Beethoven had explained that his programmatic Sixth Symphony, which he called the *Pastoral*, was 'more the expression of feeling than tone-painting', though the birdcalls which close the slow movement, the peasants' merrymaking in the scherzo, and the storm which erupts in the fourth movement, are all clearly pictorial. Berlioz, however, in his *Symphonie Fantastique*, was more direct. He supplied a detailed 'programme' for this work which, like Beethoven's *Pastoral*, is in five movements instead of the usual four. Here is a brief outline:

1. Dreams, passions A young musician with vivid imagination dreams of his beloved. In his mind she becomes a melody, an **idée fixe** (a 'fixed idea' or recurring theme) which haunts him continuously.
2. At a Ball He glimpses her among the whirling dancers at a ball as a brilliant waltz is in progress.

3. Scene in the Fields   He walks in the country. Shepherds' pipes are heard (cor anglais, oboe). He catches sight of his beloved – but she disappears from view. When the cor anglais resumes its piping there is no answering call from the oboe. Sunset; distant thunder . . .

4. March to the Scaffold   He dreams that, insane with jealousy, he has murdered his beloved and is dragged to the scaffold. (Just before the end – the *idée fixe*, followed by a vivid impression of the swift descent of the guillotine, of a head falling into the basket below.)

5. Dream of a Witches' Sabbath   He sees himself, after death, among witches and monsters. His beloved, transformed into an ugly old hag, dances and mocks at him. Funeral bells . . . chants for the dead . . .

In his *Symphonie Fantastique*, Berlioz gives the five movements a feeling of unity, of 'belonging together', by bringing in the theme which he calls the *idée fixe* at key-points throughout the Symphony – varying it each time to match the situation. Here is the beginning of the *idée fixe* as it first appears in the opening movement:

And as it is transformed into a grotesque dance in the finale:

Other composers realised the need to bring unity to the movements of a lengthy symphony. Sometimes they made use of Berlioz's device of a recurring theme – though instead of *idée fixe* they more often called it the **motto theme** (Tchaikovsky's Fifth Symphony is a good example). Sometimes two or more important themes heard earlier on in a symphony are brought back in later movements. (Dvořák, in his Ninth Symphony, 'From the New World', uses both these methods.)

Not all symphonies were of the programme type, however. The four symphonies of Brahms, for example, are absolute music, with no programmatic background at all. But in many Romantic symphonies, even though the composer makes no mention of a programme, the mood is often so intense that we feel the music must be directly based upon emotional or dramatic events which he has experienced.

The concert overture

'Overture', of course, was the name which had long been given to the orchestral piece played at the beginning of an opera. However, the 19th-century **concert overture** had no connections with opera; it was a one-movement programme piece for orchestra (usually in sonata form) simply intended for performance at a concert. Well-known concert overtures include Mendelssohn's sea-picture, *The Hebrides* (sometimes called *Fingal's Cave*), Dvořák's *Carnival Overture*, Tchaikovsky's *1812* and *Romeo and Juliet*, and Elgar's *Cockaigne*.

The symphonic poem

The **symphonic poem**, sometimes called **tone poem**, was invented by Liszt. Like the concert overture, it is a one-movement programme piece for orchestra, but is usually more lengthy and much freer in construction. Liszt's idea was that, in a symphonic poem, the music should take its shape from the pattern of ideas or events in the programme itself. To bring unity to the music, however, he used what he called **thematic transformation**. This lengthy term simply means that a basic theme recurs throughout the piece but is continually being changed, or transformed, in mood and character to match each situation (a device very similar, in fact, to Berlioz's *idée fixe*).

Liszt composed 13 symphonic poems, including *Tasso*, *Les Préludes* and *Mazeppa* (all based on poems), *Hamlet* (based on Shakespeare's play) and *Orpheus* (based on the Greek legend). Other composers soon took up the idea of writing symphonic poems, famous examples being *Danse Macabre* by Saint-Saëns, *Vltava* by Smetana, *A Night on the Bare Mountain* by Musorgsky, *The Sorcerer's Apprentice* by Dukas, and *Till Eulenspiegel* and *Don Juan* by Richard Strauss.

Assignment 63

Listen to a piece of programme music, having first discovered the 'programme' on which the composer has based his composition.
1   Which ideas in the programme come through most vividly in the music? How does the composer portray these ideas in his music?
2   Do you think it essential to know the programme in detail before listening, or would you be able to guess it from the music alone?

Incidental music

Incidental music refers to music specially composed to be heard at certain points during the performance of a play. It may set the mood at the beginning of an act or scene, entertain the audience while scenery is being changed, or even serve as background music during a scene. Since many pieces of incidental music are intentionally descriptive, they also fall into the category of programme music.

Suites

It became popular for a composer to collect together several of the pieces of incidental music he had written for a play to make a suite, intended for performance on the concert platform. Examples of this are Mendelssohn's music to Shakespeare's *A Midsummer Night's Dream*, Bizet's music for *L'Arlésienne* by Daudet, and Grieg's music for Ibsen's play, *Peer Gynt*. Another kind of suite was that made up of pieces chosen from a ballet – for instance, Tchaikovsky's suites from his ballets *Swan Lake*, *The Sleeping Beauty*, and *The Nutcracker*.

THE CONCERTO

Several changes were made to both the design and character of the concerto during the Romantic period. In the first movement, instead of the 'double exposition' found in Classical concertos, there was a single exposition – usually with the soloist entering immediately, then sharing the themes with the orchestra. The cadenza was now written out by the composer, rather than being left for the soloist to improvise. And it was more likely to be placed before, rather than after, the recapitulation section.

Although most concertos were still written in three movements, some composers tried new ideas. Mendelssohn, in his Violin Concerto, wrote linking passages to join together the three movements; Liszt designed his Second Piano Concerto as a single movement, using the technique which he called 'thematic transformation'; and Brahms composed his Second Piano Concerto in four movements, with a scherzo placed before the slow third movement.

The Romantic concerto used a large orchestra; and composers, now challenged by the brilliant technical ability of virtuoso performers, made their solo parts increasingly more difficult. Tchaikovsky, for example, made both his First Piano Concerto and his Violin Concerto so difficult that they were regarded at first as being unplayable.

The element of polite competition found in Classical concertos now became transformed into an exciting and dramatic conflict between apparently unequal forces: a single soloist opposed to the weight and power of a large orchestra. However, due to the brilliance of the player's technique and skilful writing on the part of the composer, the soloist always emerges from the battle with flying colours!

Romantic composers usually chose the piano or violin as the solo instrument in their concertos, though Schumann, Dvořák and Elgar each wrote a fine cello concerto.

Assignment 64

Listen to part of a concerto by a Romantic composer.
1 What differences do you notice between this piece and a concerto by a Classical composer?
2 Of all types of composition, the concerto is one of the most popular – with composers and audiences alike. What, do you think, might be the reasons for this?

WAGNER'S MUSIC-DRAMAS 2 ☒

In his achievements, and also in his influence on other composers, Wagner represents the most powerful musical force after Beethoven. Almost all his compositions are operas, usually based on German, or at least northern, legends. Wagner himself wrote the libretto (the words to be sung) for each one. Best known are *The Flying Dutchman*, *Lohengrin*, *Tristan and Isolde*, *The Mastersingers* – and the four operas (*The Rhinegold*, *The Valkyrie*, *Siegfried*, and *The Twilight of the Gods*) which make up the gigantic cycle called *The Ring of the Nibelung*, intended to be performed on four successive evenings.

Instead of 'operas', Wagner preferred to describe his works as **music-dramas**. His aim, he explained, was a perfect merging of all the arts of the theatre – singing, acting, costumes and scenery, lighting and stage effects. It is the orchestra, however, which provides the most important contribution to the total effect.

Wagner was a master of orchestration, creating new combinations of tone-colours and richly varied textures. His orchestra is frequently huge: a large string section, woodwind in threes, and a powerful brass section – perhaps eight horns, four trumpets, four trombones, and as many as five tubas. Percussion also plays an important part.

An orchestra as large as this, of course, can pose problems for the singers. When Wagner designed the theatre which was specially built for him at Bayreuth, he made sure that the orchestra was sunk below the level of the stage so that the singers might more easily project their voices across to the audience.

Wagner's operas are lengthy works, many taking four or five hours to perform. Instead of structuring them in individual 'numbers' (separate recitatives, arias, choruses and so on) he achieves musical and dramatic continuity by writing what he calls 'endless melody', spinning the music continuously from beginning to end of each act. Woven into the texture are many, usually short, themes which are commonly called **leading-motives** (in German: *Leitmotive*). Each one represents a character, or an emotion, perhaps an object (the gold, the sword, the ring) or a place (the river Rhine, or Valhalla, home of the gods). During the course of an opera, Wagner continually develops these motives, changing and transforming them according to the situation at the time (a process which has much in common with Berlioz's *idée fixe* and Liszt's thematic transformation).

In this example (from the Ring cycle) A shows the leading-motive representing the hero, Siegfried; B as it appears, after many other transformations, during the funeral march played after his death:

Wagner sometimes introduces leading-motives into the voice parts; more often, they are woven into the orchestral parts so that they provide a commentary on the drama or even give information about the state of mind of the various characters, revealing their hidden thoughts and feelings, reactions and intentions.

The voice parts in a Wagner opera are written in a style which combines characteristics of both recitative and aria. His melodies are based on speech rhythms, yet are lyrical and song-like, moving freely through unexpected keys. His harmonies are richly chromatic, with a powerful use of dissonance. Often, instead of resolving onto expected concords, discords will merge into further discords.

A dramatic scene from 'Siegfried'.

Assignment 65	Listen to part of an opera by Wagner; then to music by another great opera composer of the Romantic period, such as Verdi or Puccini.

Describe how each composer sets out to achieve his total effect (for example: the kind of texture, melody, and harmonies he uses; the type of orchestra, and the balance between orchestra and voices).

19TH-CENTURY NATIONALISM

By the middle of the 19th century, music had become almost completely dominated by German influences. At about this time, composers of other countries – particularly Russia, Bohemia (later to be part of Czechoslovakia) and Norway – began to feel that they should break free from these influences and discover a musical style of their own. This led to a type of Romanticism which is called **nationalism.**

We describe a composer as 'nationalist' if he deliberately aims to express strong feelings for his country in his music, or somehow brings to it a distinctive flavour by which his nationality may be easily recognised. The main ways in which he can achieve this are by making use of the folktunes or folkdance rhythms of his country, or by taking scenes from his country's life, history or legends as a basis for works such as operas or symphonic poems.

Russia

The first Russian composer to bring a national flavour into his music was Glinka in his opera *A Life for the Tsar* (1836). His lead was taken up in the 1860s by the group known as 'The Russian Five', or 'The Mighty Handful': Balakirev, Borodin, Cui, Musorgsky and Rimsky-Korsakov. Their aim was to compose in a style which was distinctly Russian in character. They worked closely together, often helping to complete and orchestrate each other's pieces. Among their best-known works, those which show the Russian nationalism spirit most strongly are Balakirev's symphonic poem, *Russia*; Borodin's opera, *Prince Igor* (which includes the barbaric and colourful Polovtsian Dances); Musorgsky's opera, *Boris Godunov*, and his symphonic poem *A Night on the Bare Mountain*; and Rimsky-Korsakov's *Scheherazade*, and his operas *The Snow Maiden* and *The Golden Cockerel*.

Bohemia

In Bohemia, Smetana was fired by the nationalist spirit, especially in his opera about Czech peasant life called *The Bartered Bride*, and his six symphonic poems entitled *Má Vlast* (My Country) based on Czech scenes, legends and history. The second piece, 'Vltava', traces the journey of a river from its source until it flows through Prague. Dvořák also wrote symphonic poems based on (frequently gruesome) Czech legends, such as *The Water Goblin* and *The Golden Spinning Wheel*. His colourful *Slavonic Dances* make use of Czech dance rhythms such as the polka and furiant, but with melodies of his own invention.

Norway

The Norwegian composer, Grieg, received his musical training in Germany, but on returning to Norway he determined to base his music on ingredients taken from Norwegian folkmusic – clearly heard in his *Norwegian Dances*, his songs, and his *Lyric Pieces* for piano.

Assignment 66

Listen to two or three pieces of music by 19th-century nationalist composers. Which ingredients does each composer make use of in order to bring a flavour of his own country to his music?

The spirit of nationalism spread to other countries – particularly Spain where Albéniz, Granados and Falla absorbed into their music ingredients from Spanish folksongs and dances. The colourful style of Spanish folkmusic had held a fascination, too, for composers of other nations, as shown in the French composer Bizet's 'Spanish' opera, *Carmen*, and the superbly orchestrated *Capriccio Espagnol* (Spanish Caprice) by the Russian composer, Rimsky-Korsakov.

19TH-CENTURY CHORAL MUSIC

The most important achievements in choral music written by Romantic composers were in the form of the oratorio and the requiem (the mass for the dead). The finest oratorios include Mendelssohn's *Elijah*, composed in the Handel tradition; Berlioz's *The Childhood of Christ*; and Elgar's *The Dream of Gerontius* which, instead of being based on a biblical text, is a setting of a religious poem.

Some of the most impressive settings of the requiem mass seem more suited to performance in a concert hall than a church. Berlioz's Requiem requires a large orchestra to which is added eight pairs of kettle drums and four extra brass groups, positioned at the four corners of the chorus and orchestra. Verdi's Requiem is dramatic (sometimes theatrical) in style but sincere in feeling. In marked contrast to both these works is the quiet and serene Requiem of the French composer, Fauré. But perhaps the finest choral work of the 19th century is Brahms's German Requiem, composed upon the death of his mother. For this work, instead of setting the usual Latin text, Brahms selects appropriate passages from the Bible.

LATE ROMANTICISM

Some composers carried the Romantic tradition on into the 20th century, two of the most important being Gustav Mahler and Richard Strauss. Both are known for their fine *Lieder*. Strauss, too, for his operas and symphonic poems; and Mahler for his huge symphonies, most of them taking well over an hour to perform.

These two composers often require gigantic forces to perform their music. Strauss's long symphonic poem, *Thus Spake Zarathustra* (1896), needs 3 flutes and piccolo, 3 oboes and cor anglais, 3 clarinets and bass clarinet, 3 bassoons and double bassoon; 6 horns, 4 trumpets, 3 trombones and 2 bass tubas; kettle drums, bass drum, triangle, cymbals, glockenspiel, a low bell in E; 2 harps, organ, and strings.

Mahler, in some of his symphonies, includes solo voices and chorus, so following the example set by Beethoven in his 'Choral' Symphony. Mahler's Eighth Symphony earned the nickname of 'Symphony of a Thousand' since, in an ideal performance, a thousand musicians take part. To a huge orchestra of 130, with extra brass seated apart, Mahler adds 8 solo voices, two large mixed choirs, and a choir of 400 children. The power of these combined forces can be overwhelming – yet there are moments, as in all Mahler's symphonies, when the orchestration is light and delicate. Whereas Strauss's style is mainly chordal, Mahler tends to weave a sinewy contrapuntal texture.

Mahler wrote his Eighth Symphony in 1906. By then, many composers were reacting against what they considered to be the excessive and over-ripe style of late Romanticism, and were already striking out in new directions – as we shall see in the next chapter.

The main characteristics of Romantic music

1. A greater freedom in form and design; a more intense and personal expression of emotion in which fantasy, imagination and a quest for adventure play an important part.
2. Emphasis on lyrical, songlike melodies; adventurous modulations; richer harmonies, often chromatic, with striking use of discords.
3. Denser, weightier textures with bold dramatic contrasts, exploring a wider range of pitch, dynamics and tone-colours.
4. Expansion of the orchestra, sometimes to gigantic proportions; the invention of the valve system leads to development of the brass section whose weight and power often dominate the texture.
5. Rich variety of types of piece, ranging from songs and fairly short piano pieces to huge musical canvasses with lengthy time-span structured with spectacular dramatic and dynamic climaxes.
6. Closer links with other arts lead to a keener interest in programme music (programme symphony, symphonic poem, concert overture).
7. Shape and unity brought to lengthy works by use of recurring themes (sometimes transformed/developed): *idée fixe* (Berlioz), thematic transformation (Liszt), leading-motive (Wagner), motto theme.
8. Greater technical virtuosity – especially from pianists and violinists.
9. Nationalism: reaction against German influences by composers of other countries (especially Russia, Bohemia, Norway).

Assignments

67 *Research* Choose five Romantic composers shown on the timechart on page 49. Find out more about their lives and music, writing a brief report on each one.

68 Room can only be found on the timechart on page 49 to include the most important Romantic composers. Give the names of others who might be added, mentioning the nationality of each composer.

69 Give an example of each of the following kinds of piece, in each case mentioning the name and nationality of the composer:
a programme symphony; a German Lied; a suite of incidental music; a Romantic opera; a symphonic poem; a Romantic piano concerto; a 19th-century choral work; a concert overture.

70 Explain each of the following:
nocturne; symphonic poem; incidental music; absolute music; étude; virtuoso; Lieder; through-composed; leading-motive; nationalism.

71 Which of the pieces you have heard seems to be most typical of 19th-century Romantic style? Listen to this music again, and describe the qualities or features which led you to choose this particular work.

72 Imagine that, at a concert, you are to listen to a Classical symphony followed by a symphony by a Romantic composer. What differences would you expect to notice between these two works?

Special Assignment C

This is another assignment requiring some musical detective-work. In the boxes below, you will find various kinds of music belonging to each of the five musical periods discussed in this book so far. Your assignment here is to listen to a varied programme of extracts taken from some of these pieces. As you listen, identify the period style of each item, and also the kind of piece being performed.

Medieval (to about 1450)
* a plainchant
* an example of organum
* a Medieval dance
* a Medieval song
* a 13th-century motet

Renaissance (1450–1600)
* a 16th-century motet or verse anthem
* a Renaissance madrigal
* a keyboard piece by a Tudor composer
* a piece for Renaissance 'dance-band'
* music from Venice in polychoral style

Baroque (1600–1750)
* a movement from a concerto grosso
* part of an oratorio
* a fugue for keyboard
* an excerpt from a Baroque opera
* a chorale prelude

Classical (1750–1810)
* a movement from a Classical sonata
* the third movement from a symphony
* an excerpt from an opera
* the finale from a string quartet
* part of a Classical concerto

Romantic (1810–1910)
* a 19th-century German Lied
* a passage from a Romantic opera
* part of a symphony or symphonic poem
* a 'character' piece for piano
* a dance by a nationalist composer

Before listening: Refresh your memory about the main characteristics of style for each period by reading the checklist at the end of each chapter. (You will also find the chart on page 73 useful in working this assignment.)

As you listen: Make a note of all the 'fingerprints' of style you discover in each piece – together with any other interesting details about the music.

After listening: Organise your findings by writing a brief report on each piece of music, mentioning:
1   The musical period during which it was composed – and, if possible, the name of the composer.
2   The type of piece, with details of the performing forces.
3   All the other 'clues' you discovered while listening to the music which helped you to make your identification.

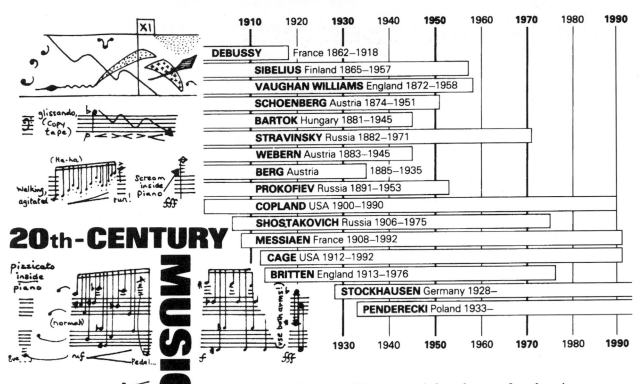

20th-CENTURY MUSIC

The story of music in the 20th century is largely one of exploration and experiment, leading to a fascinating variety of new trends, new techniques and, in some cases, entirely new sounds – all of which make this one of the most exciting periods in the history of music. As each new trend has appeared, so has a new 'label' been eagerly found to describe it, resulting in a bewildering array of '-isms' and '-alities'! As we shall find, most of these share one thing in common – a deliberate reaction to 19th-century Romantic style. This has led some critics to describe such music as 'Anti-Romantic'. The most important trends and techniques in 20th-century music include:

Impressionism	Atonality	Microtonality
20th-century Nationalism	Expressionism	Musique Concrète
	Pointillism	Electronic music
Jazz influences	Serialism	Total serialism
Polytonality	Neoclassicism	Aleatory music

Not all 20th-century composers, however, use extreme techniques. Some have continued to compose in what is basically a warm Romantic style while injecting a degree of dissonance and rhythmic vitality which clearly marks their music as belonging to the 20th century. Examples are the English composer, William Walton (especially in his concertos for viola, violin and cello) and the American composer, Samuel Barber. And there are other composers who defy classification according to any label – unless it be that of 'traditionalist', for these composers have forged a distinctive, personal style mainly based on traditions of the past. Such a composer is Benjamin Britten who has avoided following any fashionable trends and has instead

61

continued to work with basic and familiar musical materials. These he moulds and presents in new, frequently surprising, ways achieving results that are fresh, imaginative, and deeply sincere. Among his finest works are the *Serenade* for tenor voice, horn and strings; the opera, *Peter Grimes*; the *Spring Symphony*; and the *War Requiem*.

Whereas the music of each earlier period may be identified by a single overall style, common to all composers at that time, the many different trends followed by 20th-century composers result in what is really a complex mixture of styles. If we investigate four main ingredients of music, we shall find a great many characteristics, or 'fingerprints', of style which may identify a 20th-century piece:

Melodies   are likely to include wide leaps, often making use of chromatic and dissonant intervals – angular and spiky, short and fragmentary rather than long and winding; glissandi ('slidings' from one pitch to another) may be used; in some pieces, the ingredient of melody may be lacking altogether.

Harmonies   extreme dissonances, a greater proportion of discords to concords (sometimes concords may be totally avoided); note-clusters (adjacent notes played simultaneously) may be used.

Rhythms   vigorous and dynamic, with much use of syncopation (strong accents off-the-beat); unusual metres such as five or seven beats to a bar (often rooted in folkmusic); changes of metre from bar to bar; polyrhythms (*poly-* meaning 'many') – several rhythms or metres proceeding at the same time, resulting in a 'rhythmic counterpoint'; use of *ostinato* devices ('obstinately' repeated), or energetic 'motor rhythms' used to drive the music relentlessly forward.

Timbres   far greater concern with timbres (tone-colours) leading to inclusion of strange, intriguing, exotic sounds; striking, sometimes explosive, contrasts; expansion of the percussion section, and more emphasis on percussive sounds in general; unfamiliar sounds from familiar instruments, such as instruments played at the extremes of their pitch-ranges, muted brass effects, and new effects from string instruments such as bowing behind the bridge or tapping on the body of the instrument with the heel of the bow; totally new sounds, such as those involving use of electronic apparatus and magnetic tape.

2 ☷ **Assignment 73**

Listen to extracts from some of these pieces:

(a)   Stravinsky: *The Rite of Spring*
(b)   Walton: *Belshazzar's Feast*
(c)   Bartók: *Allegro barbaro*
(d)   Schoenberg: *Five Pieces for Orchestra*, Opus 16

(e)   Britten: *Peter Grimes*
(f)   Varèse: *Ionisation*
(g)   Stockhausen: *Kontakte*
(h)   Penderecki: *Threnody – To the Victims of Hiroshima*

As you listen to each piece, describe the composer's treatment of the main musical ingredients: melody, harmony, rhythm, timbre. Then arrange them in the order in which he emphasises them. (Does he, in fact, seem to *exclude* any of these ingredients?)

Let us now take a closer look at the most important trends of style
in 20th-century music. To investigate the first of these, we must
step back for a moment into the 19th century.

IMPRESSIONISM

The French conductor and composer, Pierre Boulez, has suggested that
'Modern music awakes with Debussy's *L'Après-midi d'un Faune*'. This
was Debussy's first important piece, completed in 1894, in what has
been called **Impressionist** style – a term borrowed from the style of
painting of a group of French artists known as the Impressionists.
Rather than making their paintings look 'real', as in a photograph,
these artists aimed to give merely an impression, such as the eye
might take in at a single glance: an impression of vague, hazy
outlines, and the play of shimmering light and movement.

Debussy's intention in his music at that time was to move away
from the heavy German Romantic style. The means by which he achieved
this was compared to the techniques of the Impressionist painters.
As they treated light and colour, so Debussy treated harmonies and
instrumental timbres. He used chords for their expressive, 'colour'
effects, trusting his musical instinct rather than obeying rules of
harmony so that discords merge into further discords, or similar
chords (frequently 9ths or 13ths) flow in 'chord streams' moving in
parallel motion. This brings a vague, fluid, shifting effect to
Debussy's music, heightened by his use of unusual scales: modal
scales, the five-note pentatonic scale (most easily found by playing
the black notes on the piano), or the whole-tone scale, built from
six notes a whole-tone apart (clearly heard at the beginning of the
second piano *Prélude: Voiles* – which may mean 'Sails', or 'Veils').

In his orchestral pieces, Debussy explores fresh combinations of
timbres, fluid rhythms, shimmering textures, new effects of light
and shade: avoiding hard, clearcut outlines – suggesting rather than
defining. His finest orchestral works in Impressionist style include
L'Après-midi d'un Faune, *Nocturnes*, *Images*, and *La Mer* (The Sea).

Pieces in Impressionist style by other composers include *Nights in
the Gardens of Spain* by Falla, and *The Pines of Rome* by Respighi.

9th chords, in parallel motion:

9th

Whole-tone scale on C:

*'The Houses of
Parliament' by
the Impressionist
painter Claude Monet.*

Assignment 74

Listen to a piece in Impressionist style by Debussy. Describe the various qualities of sound which make this music 'impressionistic'.

20TH-CENTURY NATIONALISM

The trend of **Nationalism** which had begun during the second half of the 19th century continued into the 20th. In America, Charles Ives made use of his country's folksongs, dance music, marching songs, popular songs and even hymns in his compositions; and Aaron Copland has included cowboy songs in his ballets *Rodeo* and *Billy the Kid*.

Some composers, such as Vaughan Williams in England and Bartók and Kodály in Hungary, took a scientific approach: collecting folktunes, then closely studying their rhythmic patterns and their melodies – often found to be based on unusual scales or modes. Sometimes these composers wrote pieces directly based upon the folktunes they had discovered – for example, Bartók's *Sonatina* (based on Transylvanian folktunes) and *Rumanian Folkdances*, Kodály's *Dances of Galánta*, and Vaughan Williams's *Five Variants of 'Dives and Lazarus'*. More often, though, they aimed to include the essential ingredients of the folkmusic they studied without quoting actual melodies. As Bartók pointed out: 'What we had to do was to discover the *spirit* of this unfamiliar music and make it the basis of our own works'. This was to become an essential element in Bartók's style, especially in works such as his *Dance Suite*, *Music for Strings, Percussion and Celesta*, and the *Sonata for Two Pianos and Percussion*.

Two other major 20th-century composers, Sibelius and Shostakovich, are nationalists in a narrower sense. Sibelius based many of his works upon Finnish legends. Although he never used folktunes, much of his music (even his seven symphonies, which are 'absolute' music) conjures up the atmosphere of his native Finland. Shostakovich has closely identified himself with his country in much of his music. His most important achievements are his fifteen symphonies, several of which portray events in Soviet history - for example, No. 7 (The 'Leningrad'), No. 11 ('The Year 1905') and No. 12 ('The Year 1917').

JAZZ INFLUENCES

Several ingredients in the general style of 20th-century music may be traced back to influences from American jazz: a fresh vitality in rhythm, often relying on strong syncopations; syncopated melodies above a steady beat; 'blue notes' – flattening certain notes of the scale such as the 3rd or 7th; muted brass effects; a keener interest in percussive sounds; and instruments playing in shrill registers.

Some composers - such as Ravel, Milhaud, Gershwin, Kurt Weill, Stravinsky, Walton and Copland - have deliberately emphasised many of these jazz ingredients in some of their works. For example: Milhaud in his ballet *La Création du Monde*; Stravinsky in *Ragtime* for eleven instruments, and *The Soldier's Tale*; and Gershwin in his *Piano Concerto*, *American in Paris*, and *Rhapsody in Blue* (which he described as a 'jazz-influenced concert-piece').

Assignment 75

Listen to one of the compositions mentioned above. Which ingredients from jazz do you hear most clearly emphasised in the music?

POLYTONALITY

Stravinsky: *Petrushka*

(2 clarinets)

When we speak of the **tonality** of a piece of music, we are referring to its *key*. In music written in C major, for instance, the ear will sense a strong 'pull' towards the most important note of that key: the *tonic* note, C. The next most important note is the dominant, G.

Some 20th-century composers have experimented with the technique of **polytonality** – writing music in two or more keys at once (if two only are involved, it is sometimes called **bitonality**). Examples of this can be heard in Stravinsky's ballets *Petrushka* and *The Rite of Spring*; in Ravel's *Bolero* where the third playing of the famous tune involves three keys at once: C, E and G; and in *Putnam's Camp* from 'Three Places in New England' by the American composer, Charles Ives (an impression of marching bands competing in different keys).

ATONALITY

Atonality means a total absence of tonality, or key. Atonal music avoids any key or mode by making free use of all twelve notes of the chromatic scale. Since all twelve notes are given equal importance, there is no pull towards any central tonic. Atonality is in fact the logical outcome of a trend which began during the Romantic period. Some composers (Wagner, in particular) had freely used chromatic discords – bringing in notes from outside the key to 'colour' the harmonies. In time, so many chromaticisms were included, together with abrupt, adventurous modulations, that there were times when the listener became uncertain which key the music was in. Gradually, tonality – the major-minor key system which had ruled Western music for almost 300 years – weakened, and began to crumble.

Certain techniques used by Debussy also helped to weaken tonality, such as discords in parallel motion, and use of the whole-tone scale. If you look at the example on page 63 you will find it is impossible to build any common chord, such as C-E-G, using notes of this scale.

All these steps led eventually to atonality, which became essential to the style of Expressionist composers.

EXPRESSIONISM

'The Scream' by Edvard Munch.

This is another term borrowed from painting – in this case from the Expressionists, working in Vienna in the early part of the century. In their vivid pictures, these painters expressed their innermost experiences and states of mind: dark, secret terrors, and fantastic visions of the subconscious – often suggesting mental breakdown.

Expressionism in music began as an exaggeration, distortion even, of late Romanticism, in which composers poured the most intense emotional expressiveness into their music. Among those who wrote in Expressionist style were Arnold Schoenberg (who was also a painter) and his pupils: Alban Berg and Anton Webern. These three, working in Vienna, became known as 'The Second Viennese School'.

In its early phase, Expressionist music relied on harmonies which became increasingly chromatic, later resulting in atonality: total rejection of key or tonality. Expressionist music in atonal style is characterised by extremely dissonant harmonies; frenzied, disjointed melodies including wild leaps; and violent, explosive contrasts with instruments often played harshly at the extremes of their ranges.

Expressionism was foreshadowed in Schoenberg's *Verklärte Nacht* 'Transfigured Night') for string sextet, written in 1899. In 1908 he composed his *Second String Quartet* in which a soprano voice is included in the third and fourth movements. It is in the fourth movement that Schoenberg totally abandons key, making the first venture into atonality. (The soprano begins, appropriately, 'I sense the air from another planet . . . I dissolve in sounds . . . ').

2 ☹ Later important atonal Expressionist works include Schoenberg's *Five Pieces for Orchestra*, Opus 16, and *Pierrot Lunaire* ('Pierrot by Moonlight') for soprano and five instrumentalists (the voice-part written in what he calls **Sprechgesang** – half spoken, half sung). Also, Berg's *Three Pieces for Orchestra*, Opus 6, and his fine opera, *Wozzeck*; and Webern's *Five Pieces for Orchestra*, Opus 10. In Webern's brief, extremely concentrated works, all instruments are treated as soloists, often playing single notes in isolation – rarely more than three or four at a time. The result is a fabric of sound which consists of scintillating dabs of instrumental colour (described by Stravinsky as Webern's 'dazzling diamonds'). This technique has been compared with that of the Pointillist artists (such as Seurat) who painted their pictures by precisely applying countless dabs, or 'points', of pure colour instead of using broad brush-strokes.

'Pointillism'

Assignment 76

Listen to an Expressionist piece by Schoenberg, Berg or Webern. What features in the music identify it as being in Expressionist style?

SERIALISM, OR 'TWELVE-NOTE' MUSIC

Having abandoned the major-minor key system in writing atonal music, Schoenberg came to realise that an entirely new principle was needed to take the place of tonality – a new procedure in composing which would bring unity and coherence to an atonal piece. His solution to this was what he called the 'twelve-note system', or **serialism.**

In writing a twelve-note composition, the composer first arranges all twelve notes of the chromatic scale in any order of his choice. This becomes the **note-row**, the basic **series**, upon which that entire composition will be based. All twelve notes are of equal importance. None should appear out of turn (though a note may occasionally be immediately repeated), but any note of the series may be used at any octave. Besides using the series in its **original** form, it may be used backwards, called **retrograde**; upside down, called **inversion**; or backwards and upside down at the same time, called **retrograde inversion**:

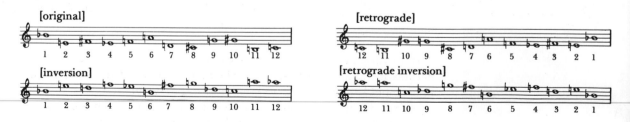

Each of these forms of the series may be transposed to begin on any note of the chromatic scale. The composer may then use any of these versions horizontally to build themes (which may be woven together contrapuntally), or the notes may be used vertically to construct chords as supporting harmonies. In any form, of course, the series provides the composer only with basic material – a series of notes. He must employ skill and imagination in the way he uses it to shape themes and construct chords, in the way he applies rhythm, in the instrumental timbres he selects, and in the textures he creates.

The series shown opposite is that devised by Schoenberg for his *Variations for Orchestra*, Opus 31. After an introduction (lasting around one and a quarter minutes, ending with a short pause) cellos begin the Theme. This consists of the series in all four versions, in the order: (1) original, (2) retrograde inversion, (3) retrograde, (4) inversion. Schoenberg transposes (2) and (4), and of course any note of the series may appear at any octave. Accompanying harmonies consist of notes of the series stacked vertically to form chords.

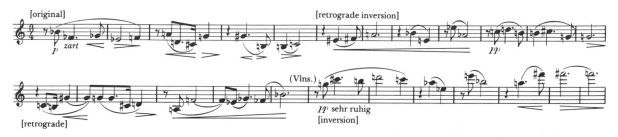

Schoenberg's pupils, Berg and Webern, also took up serialism, but in rather different ways. Berg was much freer in his approach: using notes of the series out of turn, and often bringing in extra musical material, not drawn from the series, if this seemed necessary to the effect he wished to create. He may arrange the notes in a series to imply recognisable chords in the major-minor tonal system. The series on which he bases his elegiac *Violin Concerto* begins with a chain of rising thirds, tracing four interlocking triads (G minor, D major, A minor, E major). These are topped by four notes of the whole-tone scale. This Concerto was written as a requiem in memory of a young girl who died of infantile paralysis. In the final movement of the Concerto, Berg introduces a Bach chorale (*Es ist genug*, It is enough) which begins with four whole-tones. Berg weaves his atonal music around the chorale in a way which is moving and totally convincing.

The way Berg mixes serial techniques with rich tonal harmonies is perhaps the main reason why many listeners have found his music more approachable than that of either Schoenberg or Webern.

Webern was much stricter in his use of serialism. He often aims to create perfect forms and structures similar to those he observed in certain flowers and mineral crystals. His serial works include the *Symphony*, Opus 21; the *Quartet* for clarinet, tenor saxophone, piano and violin, Opus 22; and the *Concerto* for nine instruments, Opus 24.

Assignment 77   Listen to examples of serial music by Schoenberg, Berg and Webern.
As you listen to each piece:
(a) Discover which of the main musical ingredients – melody, harmony, rhythm, timbre – are given most importance.
(b) Describe the kind of texture each composer presents in his music.

NEOCLASSICISM (THE 'NEW CLASSICISM')

Neoclassicism describes a style in 20th-century music characterised by a strong reaction to late Romanticism. Thick, congested textures for huge performing forces were replaced by a clarity of line and texture characteristic of music written before the Romantic period. The expression of intense emotion was deliberately avoided.

Some composers turned for inspiration to the Classical period proper: to the music of Haydn and Mozart. Others looked further back in time to the Baroque, taking Bach and Handel as their models, or Purcell or Monteverdi. In England, Vaughan Williams drew inspiration from the modal style of Tudor church composers (as in his *Fantasia on a Theme of Thomas Tallis* and *Mass in G minor*); Tippett integrated within his own distinctive style the springy rhythmic texture and imitative counterpoint of Elizabethan madrigal composers (as in his *Concerto for Double String Orchestra* and *Second String Quartet).*

Neoclassicism, in fact, denoted a reworking of style, forms or techniques characteristic of any period whose music pre-dated (and so was 'untainted' by) 19th-century Romanticism. Typical forms and designs 'rediscovered' by Neoclassical composers were the toccata, passacaglia, concerto grosso, fugal forms and ostinato devices. But although Neoclassical composers looked to the past for inspiration, they gave their music a very definite 20th-century flavour: abrupt modulations, sudden melodic 'twists', and piquant harmonies, often containing deliberate 'wrong notes' or making use of polytonality. 'Motor rhythms' may be used to drive the music relentlessly forward. Textures are often polyphonic rather than homophonic, with clashing dissonances throwing the separate lines of counterpoint into sharp relief. Orchestras become limited in size, presenting instrumental timbres which are sharply contrasted. Neoclassical style is often deliberately 'cool' – emphasising the sounds of wind instruments and percussion rather than the more expressive strings.

Typical works in Neoclassical style are Stravinsky's *Pulcinella* (a ballet based on tunes by Baroque composers – mainly Pergolesi), his *Concerto for Piano and Wind Instruments* and *Symphony of Psalms*; Hindemith's four Concertos, Opus 36, for piano, cello, violin, and viola, and his *Concert Music for Brass and Strings*; Poulenc's ballet *Les Biches* and his *Concert Champêtre* for harpsichord and orchestra; and many of Prokofiev's works, especially his opera *The Love of Three Oranges*, his Piano Concertos and Sonatas, and his *'Classical' Symphony* – composed, as he explained, 'as Haydn might have written it if he had lived in our day'.

Assignment 78   1   Listen to extracts from some of the compositions mentioned above. Which features of Neoclassical style do you hear in each piece?
2   In what ways may Neoclassicism be described as 'Anti-Romantic'?

NEW MATERIALS, NEW SOUNDS

Many composers have searched for new materials to incorporate into their music, often looking to the East for inspiration. For instance, the French composer, Olivier Messiaen, has made use of Hindu rhythms and metric patterns from Classical Greek poetry. He divorces these, however, from their original backgrounds and associations and uses them for his own purposes. Messiaen has also shown a fascination with the songs of birds – both those of his own country and those of more exotic places in the world. He has written down these birdsongs with the utmost precision as to rhythm and pitch, and has made them the basis for many of his compositions, such as *Réveil des Oiseaux* (The Awakening of the Birds) for piano and orchestra, *Oiseaux Exotiques* for piano and small orchestra, and *Catalogue d'Oiseaux* – thirteen pieces for piano based on the birdsongs of France.

2 ⊡ The American, John Cage, has also shown interest in both the music and the philosophies of the East. His *Sonatas and Interludes* for 'prepared' piano portray the traditional 'permanent emotions' of India, such as sorrow, mirth, fear and anger. Cage creates new sounds by 'preparing' the piano: nuts, bolts and screws, pieces of rubber and plastic, are fixed under, over and between certain strings in the piano. This affects both the timbre and pitch of those notes, producing richly varied sonorities which suggest the sounds of Eastern bells, gongs and drums.

Several composers have made similar experiments in producing new sonorities. In his *Threnody: To the Victims of Hiroshima*, the Polish composer Penderecki sometimes asks the string players to bow between the bridge and tailpiece, or on the tailpiece itself, or to strike the sounding board with the heel of the bow. In choral works, such as *St Luke Passion*, he includes, besides normal singing, muttering, speaking, whispering, shouting, hissing and whistling. Like several other 20th-century composers, Penderecki has made use in his music of note-clusters and microtones (intervals smaller than a semitone).

An entirely new range of sounds – limitless in extent – are to be found in the exploration of Musique Concrète and Electronic Music.

MUSIQUE CONCRÈTE

In the late 1940s, the French composer Pierre Schaeffer began experiments in the Studio d'Essai of French Radio in what he called *Musique Concrète* – music composed in a 'concrete' way directly onto magnetic tape rather than in an abstract way by writing notes down on paper. The sounds he recorded were natural sounds, such as a door slamming, a cork popping from a bottle, and so on. He transferred these recordings to another tape: blending them, superimposing them one on top of another, and modifying them in various ways. The pitch of a sound might be changed by altering the speed of the tape (a faster speed giving a higher pitch, a slower speed a lower pitch) or the original recorded sound might be played backwards. The resulting composition was a **montage** of sounds stored on tape which could be played back at will without need of any 'performer'.

2 ⊡ **Assignment 79**

Listen to a record of Musique Concrète. Can you identify any of the original sounds the composer has transformed in his composition?

ELECTRONIC MUSIC

Electronic music, originating in Germany in the 1950s, includes any sounds picked up by a microphone (as in Musique Concrète) and also any sounds produced from electronic sound-generators. The basic sound-producing component is an oscillator. Sounds produced may be as 'pure' (meaning free from harmonics or overtones) or as 'impure' as required. Another kind of sound is 'white noise' – a rushing sound made up of all audible frequencies.

Sounds may be electronically modified in various ways, including adjustment of volume, filtering (cutting out unwanted frequencies), or adding vibrato ('wavering'), reverberation ('delay' added so the sound dies away gradually) or echo (the sound is repeated as it dies away). Sounds may be mixed together, superimposed, or 'chopped' into separate fragments. Individual sounds may be recorded onto separate pieces of tape which are then spliced together, or a tape 'loop' may be made so sounds can be repeated to create an ostinato effect. And of course, the basic techniques of Musique Concrète play an important part, such as reversing sounds (often producing a crescendo ending with abrupt 'cut-off') and altering the pitch – though by electronic means, the pitch may change gradually with a glissando effect. The attack and/or decay of sounds may be deleted by tape editing.

An electronic composition may consist solely of electronically generated sounds, either pre-recorded on tape or manipulated 'live' before an audience. Or a composer may choose to combine the sounds with voices or instruments, sounding naturally or transformed by electronic means, live or on tape.

One of the most important composers to explore electronic music is Karlheinz Stockhausen. His electronic works include *Kontakte* for electronic sounds, piano and percussion; *Telemusik*; *Mikrophonie I* for tam-tam, 2 microphones, 2 filters, and 2 potentiometers; and *Gesang der Jünglinge* (Song of the Youths) in which a boy's voice is combined with electronic sounds. Works by other composers include *Visage for tape* (based on the voice of Cathy Berberian and electronic sounds) by Luciano Berio; and *Como una ola de fuerza y luz* ('Like a wave of force and light') by Luigi Nono. In this atmospheric work, a soprano, piano and orchestra perform 'live' in combination with a tape, previously recorded, presenting the electronically modified sounds of the soprano, piano, and a choir of female voices.

TOTAL SERIALISM

In 1949, Messiaen composed a piano piece called *Mode de Valeurs et d'Intensités* (Mode of Durations and Intensities) which he based upon scales, not only of pitch, but also of duration (note-values), dynamics and attack. This led to experiments by Messiaen and his two pupils, Boulez and Stockhausen, in **total serialism**, in which twelve-element series of pitches, durations, dynamics and attack were all totally controlled by Schoenberg's principles of serialism. Boulez was first to use total serialism in his *Structures I* for two pianos.

Stockhausen later came to believe that *any* aspect of sound could be controlled by serial procedures. His *Gruppen* (Groups) uses a scale of twelve tempi (speeds) and is played by three orchestras, widely separated in performance, each with its own conductor.

ALEATORY, OR 'CHANCE-CHOICE', MUSIC

Whereas total serialism and electronic music offer the composer greater control, **aleatory music** (from Latin, *alea*, a dice) makes for greater freedom by involving a degree of chance or unpredictability either in the composing process, in performance, or in both. The composer may take decisions about which notes to use and how to use them by throwing a dice. The performer may be required to choose between several alternatives, such as which notes or sections of the music he will play, and in which order. The pitch of notes may be indicated but not their duration, or vice versa. He may be asked to provide some notes of his own choice by improvising. In some pieces, no notes may be provided at all: merely a collection of symbols, a diagram, a drawing, or just an idea, to be freely interpreted.

Cage and Stockhausen have made much use of aleatory procedures in their music. Cage's *Imaginary Landscape No. 4* is for 12 radios, all tuned to different stations. Each radio has two 'players' – one to adjust the tuning, one to control the volume. His *Concert for Piano and Orchestra* may be performed as a solo, ensemble piece, symphony, aria (with soprano) or piano concerto. Each player chooses, in any order, any number of pages from his part. Coordination is by elapsed time, the conductor imitating with his arms the hands of a clock.

Stockhausen's *Piano Piece XI* consists of 19 sections to be played in any order. The pianist must also choose from six different tempi, dynamics and varieties of touch (staccato, legato, and so on). In his *Zyklus* (Cycle) for percussion, the single performer may begin on any page of the score, which is spirally bound and may be read clockwise, anticlockwise or even upside down. The player then follows the pages in order, ending with the first stroke of the page where he began.

Stockhausen has taken aleatory music to the extreme in what he has called 'intuitive music'. In May of 1968, he shut himself away for seven days, eating nothing but meditating deeply. From this came *Aus den Sieben Tagen: Compositions May 1968*. Here is an extract:

Ankunft – 'Arrival' (for any number of musicians)

Give up everything, we were on the wrong track.
Begin with yourself: you are a musician.
You can transform all the vibrations of the world into sounds.
If you firmly believe this, and from now on never doubt it,
    begin with the simplest exercises.

Become quite still, until you no longer think, want, feel anything.
Sense your soul, a little below your chest.
Let its radiance slowly permeate your whole body
    both upwards and downwards at the same time.
Open your head on top in the centre, a little towards the back,
    and let the current that hovers above you there,
      like a dense sphere, enter into you.
Let the current slowly fill you from head to foot and continue flowing.

Quietly, take your instrument and play, at first, single sounds.
Let the current flow through the whole instrument . . .

You will then experience everything on your own . . .

Assignments

80   Explain each of the following:
polytonality; atonality; ostinato; syncopation; whole-tone scale; note-clusters; mutes; retrograde; *Sprechgesang*; microtones.

81 A   Arrange these ten composers in the order in which they were born:
Bach; Tchaikovsky; Purcell; Britten; Beethoven; Mozart; Bartók; Byrd; Machaut; Wagner.

    B   Give each composer's nationality and mention one of his compositions.

82   Room has been found on the timechart on page 61 for only a handful of 20th-century composers. Name others who might be added to this list, mentioning each one's nationality, and one of his compositions.

83   *Research*   Choose five 20th-century composers whose music has made most impact upon you. Find out more about their lives and music, and write a brief report on each one.

84   Listen to five varied pieces of music by 20th-century composers.
(a)   Describe any typical 20th-century techniques or musical devices which you notice in each piece.
(b)   Suggest a 'label' which describes the style of the music and, if possible, identify the composer.

85   Which pieces you have heard by 20th-century composers did you find:
(a) most interesting; (b) most enjoyable; (c) most dislikable.
Give reasons for each of the choices you make.

86   Which particular trends or techniques used by 20th-century composers do you think might be developed and explored further to provide the main elements in the 'music of the future'? Why do you think future composers will find these worthy of their attention?

Special Assignment D

Listen to recordings of pieces covering all six periods of musical history – but with the items presented in a mixed historical order. (You will find the chart printed opposite helpful in working this assignment.)

Before listening: Refresh your memory about the main characteristics of style for each period by reading through the checklist included in each chapter.

As you listen: Make a note of all the 'fingerprints' of style you discover in each piece – together with any other interesting details about the music.

After listening: Write a brief report on each piece of music, mentioning:
1 The period of music during which it was composed – and, if possible, the name of the composer.
2 The type of piece, with details of the performing forces.
3 Any other 'clues' which helped you in your identification.

Suggestions for further listening

MEDIEVAL

Plainchant
Dominus dixit ad me (antiphon from the Introit to the First Christmas Mass)
Hodie Christus natus est (antiphon for Evensong on Christmas Day)
Alleluia: Pascha nostrum (alleluia for Easter Sunday)
Haec dies (gradual for Easter Sunday)
Kyrie from Mass IV ('Cunctipotens')
Veni Sponsa Christi (antiphon)

Organum
Parallel organum – *Tu patris sempiternum*
Free organum – *Cunctipotens genitor*
Melismatic organum – *Cunctipotens genitor*
Organum duplum – Léonin (attrib.): *Alleluia: Pascha nostrum* (with clausula, plus motet: *Gaudeat devotio fidelium)*

Songs
Troubadour – Giraut de Bornelh: *Reis glorios* (alba, 'dawn song'); Anon: *a l'entrada del tens clar* (ballade)
Trouvère – Guillaume d'Amiens: *Prendés i garde* (rondeau); Richard I, King of England: *Ja nus hons pris* (ballade)
Guillaume de Machaut: *Douce dame* (virelai); *Foys porter* (virelai)
Francesco Landini: *Ecco la primavera* (ballata); *Così pensoso* (pescha)
Dufay: *Se la face ay pale* (chanson)
Binchois: *Filles a marier* (chanson)

Dances
Anon. (French, 13th century): *Danse Royale; La quinte estampie Real*
Anon. (Italian, 14th century): *Saltarello; Trotto; Lamento di Tristano* and *La Rotta*

Early keyboard music
Estampies from the Robertsbridge Codex (c1325)

Motets
Anon. (French, 13th century): *Quant voi—Virgo virginum—Hec dies*
Anon. (English, 13th century): *Alle, psallite cum luya* (using voice-exchange)
Machaut: *De bon espoir—Puis que la douce* (isorhythmic)
Dunstable: *Sancta Maria* (using fauxbourdon style); *Veni Sancte Spiritus* (isorhythmic)
Dufay: *Ave regina coelorum* (using fauxbourdon style)

Mass
Machaut: Kyrie from *Messe de Notre Dame* (plainchant cantus firmus)
Dufay: Kyrie from Mass: *Se la face ay pale* (secular cantus firmus)

Rota (round, canon)
Sumer is icumen in (c1240)

Music-drama
Anon: *The Play of Daniel*

Other instrumental
Machaut: *Hoquetus David* (instrumental hocket)
Anon. (French, 14th century): *Le Moulin de Paris* (variations)
Dunstable: 'Puzzle Piece' (Puzzle Canon III)

RENAISSANCE

Motet
Josquin des Prez: *Ave Maria*
Palestrina: *Exsultate Deo*
Byrd: *Haec dies*
Victoria: *Ave Maria*
Sweelinck: *Hodie Christus natus est*
Monteverdi: *Exultent caeli*

Mass
Josquin: Sanctus from *Missa L'homme armé (super voces musicales)*
Taverner: Benedictus from Mass: *Gloria tibi Trinitas*

	Palestrina: Kyrie from *Missa Brevis*; Kyrie and Agnus Dei from *Missa 'Veni Sponsa Christ'* Byrd: Agnus Dei from *Mass for Four Voyces*

Carols and partsongs
Nowell syng we (15th century); Agincourt Carol – *Deo gratias Anglia* (1415)
Henry VIII: *Pastyme with good companye*
Cornyshe: *Ah, Robin*

Italian madrigals
Monteverdi: *O primavera*; *Si ch'io vorrei morire*; *Zefiro torna*
Gesualdo: *Mille volte il di moro*; *Moro lasso*

English madrigals
Bennet: *All creatures now are merry-minded*
Byrd: *This sweet and merry month of May*
Gibbons: *The Silver Swan*
Morley: *Sing we and chant it* (ballett)
Weelkes: *Sing we at pleasure* (ballett)
Dowland: Ayres – *Come again sweet love*; *Fine knacks for ladies*; *My thoughts are wing'd with hope*

Anthems
Full – Tallis: *If Ye Love Me*
      Byrd: *Sing joyfully*
Verse – Gibbons: *This is the Record of John*
       Gibbons: *Behold, Thou has made my days*

Polychoral style
Lassus: Ten-part madrigal – *Trionfi del Tempo*
Giovanni Gabrieli: Twelve-part motet – *Angelus ad Pastores*; fourteen-part motet – *In Ecclesiis* (solo voices, double chorus and instruments); *Canzon Septimi Toni* for two instrumental groups; *Canzon: 'Sol sol la sol fa mi'* for two instrumental groups; *Sonata pian' e forte*

English consort music
Byrd: *Fantasia for a consort of viols*
Holborne: *The Honie Suckle*
Gibbons: *In nomine*
Byrd: *Monsieurs Alman*

Dance-music
Anon: Basse danse – *La Spagna*
Susato: Basse-danse – *La Mourisque*; Pavane – *La Bataille*
Praetorius: Dances from 'Terpsichore'

Elizabethan keyboard music
Anon: *My Lady Careys Dompe* (ground); Anon: *Branle Hoboken*
Taverner: *In nomine* (for organ)
Byrd: *Watkins Ale*; *The Carmans Whistle*
Bull: *A Gigge – Doctor Bull's My Selfe*; *The Princes Coranto*
Gibbons: *The Queenes Command*; Pavan and Galliard – *The Earl of Salisbury*
Farnaby: *A Toye*; *Giles Farnaby's Dream*; *His Rest*; *Muscadin*
Anon: *Coranto* from 'Parthenia Inviolata' (virginals, with bass viol)

BAROQUE

Monody
Caccini: *Dolcissimo sospiro* (from *Le Nuove Musiche*)

Opera
Monteverdi: *Orfeo*, Act II: 'In un fiorito prato' (Messenger)—'Tu se' morta' (Orfeo's lament)—'Ahi, case acerbo' (Chorus); Act III: 'Possente spirto' (virtuoso aria for Orfeo)
Purcell: *Dido and Aeneas*
Rameau: Dances from *Les Indes Galantes* (opéra-ballet)
Handel: *Giulio Cesare* – aria: 'V'adoro pupille'. *Alcina* – recitative (secco): 'Tanto mi è grato', and aria: 'Di cor mio'; arias: 'Sta nell'Ircana' and 'Verdi prati'

Overture
French style – Purcell: Overtures to *Dido and Aeneas* and *The Indian Queen*
Italian style – Boyce: Overture to the *Ode for New Year*, 1756 (Boyce later published the same music as the first of his 'Eight Symphonys')

Oratorio	Handel: *Israel in Egypt* – 'He spake the word' (double chorus); 'But as for His people' (chorus). *Judas Maccabaeus* – 'Father of Heaven' (alto aria); choruses: 'See, the conquering hero comes' and 'Hallelujah, Amen'
Mass	Bach: Mass in B minor – Osanna and Benedictus; Et resurrexit; Agnus Dei
Anthems	Purcell: *Hear my prayer, O Lord*; *Rejoice in the Lord alway* Handel: *Zadok the Priest*
Cantata	Schütz: *Saul, Saul, was verfolgst du mich?* Bach: Cantata No. 11 – *Lobet Gott*; No. 50 – *Nun ist das Heil*
Fugue	Bach: Prelude and Fugue in F minor ('The 48', Book II); Chromatic Fantasia and Fugue; Toccata and Fugue in D minor (BWV 565) for organ; Passacaglia and Fugue in C minor for organ
Chorale Prelude	Bach: *Ich ruf' zu dir, Herr Jesu Christ*; *In dulci jubilo*
Suite	Handel: Keyboard Suite No. 5 in E; *Music for the Royal Fireworks* Bach: French Suite No. 5 in G; Orchestral Suite No. 2 in B minor
Trio Sonata	Purcell: Trio Sonata No. 9 in F, 'Golden' (sonata da chiesa) Couperin: *La Françoise*, from 'Les Nations' (sonata da camera)
'Solo' Sonata	Tartini: Sonata in G minor, 'The Devil's Trill', for violin and continuo Handel: Sonata in G minor, Opus 1 No. 2, for recorder and continuo Bach: Sonata in B minor for flute and continuo
Harpsichord Sonata	Domenico Scarlatti: Sonata in D minor, 'Pastorale' (L413; K9); in A minor (L429; K175); in D (L164; K491); in G (L349; K146); in A major (L495; K24); in F (L279; K419); in E, 'Cortège' (L23; K380)
Concerto Grosso	Corelli: Opus 6 No. 8 in G minor ('Christmas'); No. 7 in D; No. 12 in F Vivaldi: Opus 3 No. 2 in G minor; Opus 3 No. 11 in D minor Handel: Opus 3 No. 1 in B♭; Opus 6 No. 6 in G minor and No. 10 in D minor Bach: Brandenburg Concertos Nos. 1 and 2
Solo Concerto	Vivaldi: Violin Concerto 'Spring' from *The Four Seasons* Handel: Oboe Concerto No. 3 in G minor; Harp Concerto in B♭, Opus 4 No. 6 Bach: Harpsichord Concerto No. 5 in F minor; Violin Concerto in E major

CLASSICAL

Sonata	C.P.E. Bach: Sonata in F minor (Wq 57 No. 6) Haydn: Piano Sonata in D (H37; L50); Piano Sonata in G minor (H44; L32) Mozart: Piano Sonata in A, K331; in B♭, K333; Violin Sonata in G, K301 Beethoven: Piano Sonata No. 8 in C minor (*Pathétique*); No. 14 in C♯ minor ('Moonlight'); No. 21 in C ('Waldstein'); No. 23 in F minor ('Appassionata'); Violin Sonata No. 5 in F ('Spring')
Symphony	Stamitz: Symphony in D, Opus 3 No. 2; in E♭ (*La Melodia Germanica* No. 3) J.C. Bach: Symphony in D, Opus 18 No. 3, for double orchestra Haydn: Symphony No. 6 in D (*Le Matin*); No. 31 in D ('Hornsignal'); No. 45 in F♯ minor ('Farewell'); No. 94 in G ('Surprise'); No. 104 in D ('London') Mozart: Symphony No. 29 in A; No. 32 in G (in the style of an Italian overture); No. 39 in E♭; No. 40 in G minor; No. 41 in C ('Jupiter') Beethoven: Symphony No. 2 in D; No. 3 in E♭ ('Eroica'); No. 5 in C minor; No. 6 in F (*Pastoral*); No. 7 in A; No. 9 in D minor ('Choral')
Concerto	C.P.E. Bach: Concerto for harpsichord, fortepiano and orchestra Haydn: Cello Concerto in D; Trumpet Concerto in E♭

Mozart: Piano Concerto No. 17 in G, K453; No. 20 in D minor, K466; Horn Concertos; Clarinet Concerto in A

Beethoven: Piano Concerto No. 3 in C minor; No. 4 in G; No. 5 in E♭ ('Emperor'); Violin Concerto in D

Sinfonia Concertante

Haydn: Sinfonia Concertante in B♭ (oboe, bassoon, violin, cello, and orchestra)

Mozart: Sinfonia Concertante in E♭ (violin, viola, and orchestra)

Chamber music

Haydn: String Quartet in C, Opus 33 No. 3 ('Bird'); in D, Opus 64 No. 5 ('Lark'); in C, Opus 76 No. 3 ('Emperor'); in G minor, Opus 74 No. 3 ('Rider'); Piano Trio No. 25 in G ('Gypsy Rondo')

Mozart: String Quartet in D minor, K421; in C, K465 ('Dissonance'); Clarinet Quintet; String Quintet in G minor; Trio in E♭ for piano, clarinet, and viola

Beethoven: String Quartet in D, Opus 18 No. 3; in F, Opus 59 No. 1 ('Razumovsky' No. 1); Wind Sextet in E♭, Opus 71; Septet in E♭, Opus 20; Octet in E♭, Opus 103

Divertimento, Serenade

Mozart; Divertimento No. 1 in E♭, K113; Serenade No. 6 in D, K239 (*Serenata Notturno*); No. 10 in B♭, K361, for 13 wind instruments

Overture

Mozart: Overtures to *The Marriage of Figaro, Don Giovanni, The Magic Flute, The Abduction from the Seraglio*

Beethoven: 'Egmont' Overture; Overture to *Fidelio*

Opera

Gluck: *Orfeo ed Euridice*, Act II

Mozart: *The Marriage of Figaro*, Act I (Nos. 6–9); *Don Giovanni* - 'Là ci darem la mano'; 'Or sai chi l'onore'; and Finale to Act II

Beethoven: *Fidelio* – Quartet: 'Mir ist so wunderbar'; Prisoners' Chorus: 'O welche Lust'

Oratorio

Haydn: *The Creation* – recitative: 'And God said' and aria: 'With verdure clad'; Chorus: 'The heavens are telling'

Mass

Mozart: Requiem aeternam, Kyrie, and Lacrymosa, from Requiem in D minor

Beethoven: Santus and Benedictus, from 'Missa Solemnis' in D major

ROMANTIC

Lieder

Schubert: *Im Frühling*; *Der Doppelgänger*; *Der Tod und das Mädchen*; *An die Laute*; *An den Mond* ('Geuss, lieber Mond'); *Ständchen*; *Am Meer*

Schumann: *Widmung*; *Die beiden Grenadiere*; *Der Nussbaum*; *Die Lotusblume*

Brahms: *Feldeinsamkeit*; *Ständchen*; *Regenlied*; *Liebesliederwalzer*

Wolf: *Storchenbotschaft*; *Denk es, O Seele*; *Der Feuerreiter*

Mahler: *Des Antonius von Padua Fischpredigt*; *Rheinlegendchen*

Strauss: *Ständchen*; *Morgen*; *Schlechtes Wetter*

Song cycles

Schubert: *Die Schöne Müllerin*

Schumann: *Dichterliebe*

Mahler: *Lieder eines fahrenden Gesellen*

Piano pieces

Schubert: Impromptu in A♭ (Opus 90/4); Moments Musicaux (Opus 94) 3 and 6

Mendelssohn: *Songs without Words* – No. 18 in A♭ ('Duet'), No. 25 in G ('May Breezes'), No. 34 in C ('Spinning Song')

Chopin: Fantaisie-Impromptu; Nocturne in F♯ Opus 15 No. 2 and in D♭ Opus 27 No. 2; Waltz in D♭ Opus 64 No. 1 ('Minute') and in C♯ minor Opus 64 No. 2; Mazurka in B♭ Opus 7 No. 1, in A minor Opus 7 No. 2; Étude in E Opus 10 No. 3, in C minor Opus 10 No. 12 ('Revolutionary'), in A minor Opus 25 No. 11 ('Winter Wind'); Polonaise in A ('Military'); Ballade No. 1 in G minor

Schumann: Romance No. 2 in F♯; *Papillons*; *Carnaval*

Liszt: Études – *La Campanella* and *La Chasse* (both based on violin pieces by Paganini); Hungarian Rhapsodies 2 and 11; *En Rêve* (Nocturne)

Brahms: Ballade in D minor Opus 10 No. 1 and in G minor Opus 118 No. 3; Romance in F Opus 118 No. 5; Rhapsody in E♭ Opus 119 No. 4

Symphonies	Schubert: Symphony No. 8 in B minor ('Unfinished') Berlioz: *Romeo and Juliet* – Feast of the Capulets, Love Scene Mendelssohn: Symphony No. 4 in A (*Italian*) Liszt: *Faust Symphony* (using the device of thematic transformation) Franck: Symphony in D minor (in cyclic form) Bruckner: Symphony No. 7 in E Brahms: Symphony No. 2 in D Tchaikovsky: Symphony No. 6 in B minor (*Pathétique*) Dvořák: Symphony No. 8 in G Mahler: Symphony No. 3 (movements 2, 3, 5)
Concert overtures	Berlioz: *Le Carnaval Romain* Mendelssohn: *A Calm Sea and a Prosperous Voyage* Brahms: *Academic Festival Overture*; *Tragic Overture*
Symphonic poems (tone poems)	Liszt: *Les Préludes* Smetana: *Šárka* (from 'Má Vlast') Borodin: *In the Steppes of Central Asia* Tchaikovsky: *Francesca da Rimini* Strauss: *Don Juan*; *Ein Heldenleben*
Concertos	Mendelssohn: Violin Concerto in E minor Liszt: Piano Concerto No. 1 in E♭ Brahms: Violin Concerto; Double Concerto for violin, cello and orchestra Grieg: Piano Concerto in A minor
Sonatas	Chopin: Piano Sonata No. 2 in B♭ minor Liszt: Piano Sonata in B minor (in one movement) Brahms: Violin Sonata No. 1 in G Franck: Violin Sonata in A
Chamber music	Schubert: Piano Quintet in A ('The Trout'); Octet in F Smetana: String Quartet in E minor ('From my life') Brahms: Clarinet Quintet; Trio in E♭ for piano, violin and horn Dvořák: Piano Quintet in A; Bagatelles for two violins, cello, harmonium
Opera	Wagner: *Das Rheingold* (final moments of final scene); *Tristan und Isolde* – Prelude and Liebestod Verdi: *Rigoletto* – 'Caro nome'; 'La donna è mobile'; 'Bella figlia dell'amore' (quartet); *La Traviata* – Brindisi (drinking song); 'Addio del passato' Smetana: *The Bartered Bride* – Overture; opening chorus; Polka Puccini: *Tosca*, Act III; *La Bohème*, Act I

'MODERN' (20th CENTURY)

Debussy	*Prelude à 'L'Après-midi d'un Faune'*; *La Mer*; 'Nuages' (from *Fêtes*)
Sibelius	Symphony No. 4 in A minor; Symphony No. 7 in C; *Tapiola* (symphonic poem)
Vaughan Williams	*Fantasia on a Theme by Thomas Tallis*; Symphony No. 6 in E minor
Ives	Piano Sonata No. 2, 'Concord' (movements 2 and 3); *The Unanswered Question*; *The Fourth of July* (from 'New England Holidays'); *Putnam's Camp* (from 'Three Places in New England')
Schoenberg	*Pierrot Lunaire* (Nos. 1–5); String Quartet No. 2 (fourth movement); *Five Orchestral Pieces*, Opus 16; *Variations for Orchestra*, Opus 31

Ravel	*Introduction and Allegro* (Septet); *Daphnis et Chloé*; Piano Concerto in G
Bartók	*Allegro barbaro*; String Quartet No. 4; *Music for Strings, Percussion and Celesta*; Sonata for Two Pianos and Percussion; Concerto for Orchestra; Sonata for Solo Violin; Piano Concerto No. 3
Stravinsky	*Petrushka*; *The Rite of Spring*; *Ragtime*; *L'Histoire du Soldat*; *Pulcinella*; *Symphony of Psalms*; *Concerto for 15 Instruments* ('Dumbarton Oaks')
Webern	*Five Movements for Strings*, Opus 5; *Six Pieces for Orchestra*, Opus 6; *Five Pieces for Orchestra*, Opus 10; Symphony, Opus 21; Concerto, Opus 24
Varèse	*Ionisation*; *Déserts* (orchestra and prepared tape); *Poème Électronique*
Berg	*Three Pieces for Orchestra*, Opus 6; Chamber Concerto; *Wozzeck* – Act 1 Scene 3, Act III Scenes 4 and 5
Prokofiev	*Romeo and Juliet*; Symphony No. 1 ('Classical'); Piano Concerto No. 3
Milhaud	*La Création du Monde*
Orff	*Carmina Burana*
Hindemith	Symphony: *Mathis der Maler*; *Kammermusik No. 2* Opus 24/2
Gershwin	*Rhapsody in Blue*; *An American in Paris*
Copland	*Appalachian Spring*; *Rodeo*; Clarinet Concerto
Tippett	*Fantasia on a Theme of Corelli*; Concerto for Orchestra; Symphony No. 3
Shostakovich	Symphony No. 5; Symphony No. 7 ('Leningrad')
Messiaen	*Oiseaux Exotiques*; *Et exspecto Resurrectionem Mortuorum*; *La Nativité du Seigneur* for organ (Nos. 4 and 6); *Quatuor pour la fin du temps*
Cage	Sonata 2 from *Sonatas and Interludes* for 'prepared' piano; *Fontana Mix*
Lutoslawski	*Jeux Vénitiens*; *Musique Funèbre* (in memory of Bartók)
Britten	*Variations on a Theme of Frank Bridge*; *A Ceremony of Carols*; *Peter Grimes*; *Spring Symphony*; *Noyes Fludde*; *War Requiem*
Xenakis	*ST/4* for string quartet (calculated on IBM computer); *Polytope* (for four orchestras 'scattered throughout the audience')
Ligeti	*Volumina* (organ); *Lux Aeterna* (voices); *San Francisco Polyphony* (orchestra)
Nono	*Coma una ola de fuerza y luz* for piano, soprano, orchestra and tape
Boulez	*Le Marteau sans Maître*
Berio	*Sequenza III* for female voice; *Différences*; *Sinfonia*
Stockhausen	*Gesang der Jünglinge* (electronic); *Gruppen* for three orchestras (total serialism); *Zyklus* for percussion (aleatory); *Kontakte* for piano, percussion and electronic tape; *Mixtur* for five orchestral groups, sine-wave generators and ring modulators
Penderecki	*Threnody: To the Victims of Hiroshima*; *Stabat Mater*; Symphony No. 1
Birtwhistle	*Chronometer*
Maxwell Davies	*Eight Songs for a Mad King*; Symphony No. 1
Steve Reich	*Music for mallet instruments, voices and organ*

Index